Journal of the
GRACE EVANGELICAL SOCIETY
"Faith Alone in Christ Alone"

| VOLUME 31 | Autumn 2018 | NUMBER 61 |

Journal of the
GRACE EVANGELICAL SOCIETY
Published Semiannually by GES

Editor
Kenneth W. Yates

Associate Editors
Robert N. Wilkin
Shawn Lazar

Layout
Shawn Lazar

Manuscripts, book reviews, and other communications should be addressed to GES, Director of Publications, P.O. Box 1308, Denton, TX 76202 or submissions@faithalone.org.

Journal subscriptions, renewals, and changes of address should be sent to the Grace Evangelical Society, P.O. Box 1308, Denton, TX 76202 or email ges@faithalone.org. Subscription Rates: single copy, $9.25 (U.S.); 1 year, $18.50; 2 years, $35.00; 3 years, $49.50; 4 years, $62.00; $13.50 per year for active full-time students. Please add $4.00 for US shipping. Add $4.50 per year for shipping to Mexico and Canada and $8.50 per year for all other international shipping. New subscriptions, 1 year, $9.25; gift subscriptions, 1 year, $9.25.

Purpose: Grace Evangelical Society was formed "to promote the clear proclamation of God's free salvation through faith alone in Christ alone, which is properly correlated with and distinguished from issues related to discipleship."

We Affirm: God, out of love for the human race, sent the Lord Jesus Christ into the world to save sinners. He paid the full penalty for human sin when He died on the cross. Any person who believes in Jesus Christ for everlasting life receives that gift which, as the words *everlasting life* suggest, can never be lost (John 1:29; 3:16-18; 19:30; 1 Tim 1:16).

Third-class postage has been paid at Dallas, Texas. Postmaster: Send address changes to Grace Evangelical Society, P.O. Box 1308, Denton, TX 76202

THE CHURCH: CHOSEN TO REIGN (EPHESIANS 1:4-5)

KENNETH W. YATES

Editor

I. INTRODUCTION

Paul uses two verbs in Eph 1:4-5 which deal directly with the issue of election. In the NKJV, the verbs are "to choose" and "to predestine." The Apostle writes:

> …just as He *chose* us in Him before the foundation of the world, that we should be holy and without blame before Him in love, having *predestined* us to adoption as sons by Jesus Christ to Himself, according to the good pleasure of His will… (emphasis added)

R. C. Sproul cites these verses, along with eleven others, and concludes that if an exegete is going to be Biblical, the issue is not whether the Bible teaches predestination or not, but what kind of predestination is Biblical.[1] Sproul makes it clear that he strongly believes that God has predestined or chosen certain individuals for eternal life. This choice was made by God before these people were born. Their eternal destinies were settled even before the world was created. Sproul goes on to say that to believe otherwise is to make eternal salvation dependent upon work and makes the person holding that view an Arminian.[2] This, in turn, would deny that eternal salvation is completely by the grace of God.

This article will agree with Sproul that Eph 1:4-5 does teach predestination. However, it will disagree that this predestination involves God's selecting specific individuals for eternal life. Instead, it involves the corporate Church and the service God has called the Church to do.

---

[1] R. C. Sproul, *Chosen by God* (Wheaton, IL: Tyndale House Publishers, 1986), 11.

[2] Ibid., 13.

It would be helpful to look at how different scholars view the doctrine of election. It will become clear that one could disagree with Sproul's definition and still hold to salvation by grace through faith alone.[3]

II. DIFFERENT VIEWS OF ELECTION

Some agree with Sproul that in Eph 1:4-5 Paul is teaching that God has chosen some people for eternal life before they were born. Among those who do agree, there are differences of opinion as to when this choosing took place and whether this choosing by God removes all free will. Others believe that the predestination of Ephesians 1 does not involve the choosing of individuals but the Church.

A. Individual Election Without Free Will

There are many who would agree with Sproul that God has chosen who will spend eternity with Him. This all happened before they were born. God's will cannot be thwarted; thus, this view involves the removal of any free will on the part of men and women. Since God chose certain people to be eternally saved, they have no choice but to believe. Those not chosen will not believe. Man does not have free will in this matter.

All who hold this view would appeal to Eph 1:4-5. They could be divided into two groups. Some within both groups hold that God also chose who would spend eternity in the lake of fire (double predestination). Others believe that God only chose who would have eternal life and that those He did not chose were not involved in any choosing. They were eternally damned to begin with and simply remain in that state. God left them as they were.

---

[3] Of course, Sproul and those who accept his definition of divine election would contend that this very sentence argues against salvation by grace alone. They maintain that faith is itself a work and involves man's participation in his eternal salvation. However, it is not necessary to see faith as a work. Faith occurs when a person simply believes in the promise of eternal life as a free gift from Christ. Believing the promise of a free gift is not a work and does not mean the believing person is working to obtain that gift. It seems that it is only in the area of theological discussion that it would be suggested that believing the offer of a free gift is a work.

1. Supralapsarianism

Supralapsarianism maintains that God decreed mankind would fall into sin in the Garden of Eden. The election of certain people for eternal salvation *logically* preceded this decree.[4] It only logically preceded God's decree that Adam and Eve would sin because God has always known everything and therefore has always decreed everything. Mankind had no free will when they sinned in the Garden, and the elect have no free will when they believe the gospel today.

Reymond argues for a supralapsarian view. He states that God placed at the "forefront" of His plans the salvation by Christ of certain men and women. He did it even before He decreed they would sin. The salvation of these people was done in such a way that God arranged all the means to achieve that salvation. This would include even the fall of man into sin.[5]

Reymond refers to Eph 1:4-5, along with Eph 1:9, 11, to support this view. These verses, he suggests, show that the eternal salvation of specific individuals "proceeds from the pure sovereignty and absolute determination of His [God's] counsel." Such election is both "unconditional" and "unconditioned" and dependent solely upon the grace of God. Ephesians 1:4-5 teaches us that "from all eternity" God has chosen a course of action that would result in the eternal salvation of His children.[6]

Reymond believes so strongly in the impossibility of any free will on man's part in his salvation that he says no Christian can "legitimately doubt" a supralapsarian view of Eph 1:4-5. He points out that other scholars of weight agree with this assessment.[7]

---

[4] Frank Cross and Elizabeth Livingston, eds., "Supralapsarianism," in *The Oxford Dictionary of the Christian Church* (New York, NY: Oxford University Press, 2005), 1563.

[5] Robert L. Reymond, "A Consistent Supralapsarian Perspective on Election," in *Perspectives on Election: 5 Views*, ed. Chad Owen Brad (Nashville, TN: B & H Academic, 2006), 150.

[6] Ibid., 160-61.

[7] Ibid., 161. Reymond quotes approvingly from John Murray, "The Plan of Salvation," in *Collected Writings of John Murray* (Edinburgh: Banner of Truth, 1977), 2:127.

2. Infralapsarianism

Infralapsarianism agrees with advocates of supralapsarianism in that God chose certain people to obtain eternal life and that mankind has no free will in this matter. However, they disagree as to when this decree to save certain people logically occurred. The election of the saved followed the decree of the fall of man in the Garden.[8]

Ware holds to an infralapsarian view and says that all of Paul's long introduction in Eph 1:3-14 supports it. If man had free will, there would be an element of uncertainty about the eternal salvation of the elect of God. However, in Eph 1:3, Paul begins the introduction with praising God for what He has done for His children in blessing them in every way (vv 6, 12 also mention praise to God). Any uncertainty would undermine the praise that God receives. The whole tenor of Eph 1:3-14 clearly states that all Paul is speaking of is the result of God's counsel and election. God's choice of the individuals He saves is His choice, "pure and simple."[9] God completely controls who is saved and who is not.[10]

Ephesians 1:11 mentions the "inheritance" that those chosen by God receive. This inheritance is the eternal salvation of individuals, the elect sinners.[11] The goal of this election is that the individuals chosen by God would be "holy and blameless." This refers to what Christ has done through His saving work on the cross for those pre-destined by God. They were chosen to be conformed to the likeness of Christ in perfect holiness.[12] Both Reymond and Ware maintain this refers to what the elect will be forever in the presence of God.

3. Other Reformed Views

Others who hold that Paul is speaking of election to eternal life of individuals as well as the fact that mankind does not have free will in that salvation do so without specifically taking on a supralapsarian or infralapsarian understanding. Hodge says that Eph 1:4-5 speaks of

[8] Cross and Livingston, *Oxford Dictionary*, 1563.

[9] Bruce A. Ware, "Divine Election to Salvation: Unconditional, Individual, and Infralapsarian" in *Perspectives on Election: 5 Views* (Nashville, TN: B & H Academic, 2006), 13.

[10] Ibid., 23.

[11] Ibid., 14.

[12] Ibid., 51, 58.

predestination of individuals for eternal salvation. This is the heavenly "inheritance" of every believer (v 11).[13]

Hodge notes that in Eph 1:12-13, Paul speaks in a corporate sense. "We who first trusted in Christ" (v 12) refers to all Jewish believers. "In Him you also trusted" refers to Gentile believers (v 13). Even though this is the case, Hodge says that Paul is not talking about the election of the Church made up of such Jewish and Gentile believers. There is no corporate election.[14]

Also of interest is Hodge's view that the holiness mentioned in v 4 does not deal only with the holiness one has as a result of being "in Christ." That is the emphasis, but the believer is also to walk in holiness. Daily living in holiness is also the evidence of being chosen by God to eternal salvation.[15]

Calvin agrees that God's predestination in Ephesians 1 concerns His choosing of individuals for eternal life and that to hold any other view is an exercise in changing the gospel. Even though it sounds unfair and paints a picture of God we do not like, we must accept it. In addition, election in this sense takes all glory away from man and gives it to God.[16]

However, like Hodge, Calvin asserts that the holiness in v 4 contains an element of how a Christian lives in this life and not simply the positional holiness the believer has by being in Christ. When Paul says that believers are to be holy and blameless before Christ "in love," the love does not refer to the love of God that chose certain believers for the kingdom, but the love that is to be manifested between believers. Like Hodge, Calvin says that Christian love is a display of the believer's election. God's election to eternal life does not make us holy in daily living, but election and holy living go hand in hand.[17]

Hoehner also takes a Reformed view of election in Eph 1:4-5 but softens possible objections by saying that God's election of certain individuals is not cruel because He was not obligated to choose

---

[13] Charles Hodge, *A Commentary on the Epistle to the Ephesians* (Grand Rapids, MI: Eerdmans, 1950), 55.

[14] Ibid., 30.

[15] Ibid., 34-35.

[16] John Calvin, *Sermons on the Epistle to the Ephesians* (Carlisle, PA: The Banner of Truth, 1973), 25-26.

[17] Ibid., 33-37.

anybody. It was gracious that He chose any at all. In addition, Paul does not say that God chose some for an eternal hell.[18]

Those chosen receive eternal life. This is an individual and not a corporate election. Hoehner says that the plural "us" in vv 4-5 simply refers to Paul and every single believer at Ephesus. This is true for every believer because he is in Christ/Him (vv 3-4).[19] God chose the believer before the world was created by Him. One's eternal destiny is determined before he is born. God chose the believer (v 4) because He predestined (v 5) his destiny. The believer has been predestined for "adoption" (v 5), which means the believer is now a son of God. He is no longer under his old father Satan but in the family of God.[20]

While the holiness of v 4 refers to what the believer will be in the kingdom of God, Hoehner says it also refers to current Christian living. He agrees with Hodge and Calvin that "in love" refers to the love between humans and not God's love for the elect.[21]

Pink also sees the election and predestination of Eph 1:4-5 in individual terms. To be holy and blameless "before Him" in v 4 refers to our status before God in Christ.[22] This perfect holiness refers to the world to come but it also refers to the believer's imperfect holiness in this world. Here Pink agrees with the doctrine of the perseverance of the saints. He states that God does not choose a person for eternal life in eternity past without making him holy in this life as well, even if this present holiness is "imperfect." If this type of temporary holiness is not present, the professed Christian will not be a part of the kingdom of God since he has a false faith.[23]

Hendriksen takes a view very similar to Pink's. The election of Eph 1:4 deals with individual believers, even though Paul applies it to the believers at Ephesus. God predestines the individual believer to be His child, and He does it "in love." However, the inheritance (v 11) of the believer is not simply being a part of the kingdom of God and

---

[18] Harold W. Hoehner, *Ephesians: An Exegetical Commentary* (Grand Rapids, MI: Baker Academic, 2002), 176.

[19] Ibid., 177.

[20] Ibid., 178, 192-96.

[21] Ibid., 179-84.

[22] A. W. Pink, *The Doctrines of Election and Justification* (Grand Rapids, MI: Baker Book House, 1975), 77.

[23] Ibid., 78.

that "future glory." It also includes the present blessings involved with being in Christ.[24]

Being holy and without blame, for Hendriksen, also has a future and present component. God begins it in this life but it finds its ultimate reality in the world to come. Even in the present age it is always true, as far as the Christian is concerned, in God's sight.[25]

Simpson takes up this theme of holy living. Not only are individual believers elected to eternal life and stamped with the image of Christ as adopted sons of God, they are elected to holiness. Eternal life as well as holy living, or sanctification, is guaranteed for all God has chosen. Simpson argues that "in love" in v 4 modifies "holy and without blame." He seems to indicate that God's predestination of believers also guarantees that they will love one another.[26]

It should be noted, however, that Simpson acknowledges a corporate aspect in the passage. The "we" and "you" in vv 12-13 refer to Jewish and Gentile believers respectively who make up the church at Ephesus.[27]

B. Individual Election with Free Will

Both Chafer and Ironside are Dispensationalists who believe that Eph 1:4-5 speak of God's choosing individual people for eternal life. However, they differ from the previously discussed group, for they say that men and women still have the freedom to believe or not to believe.

Chafer says that everyone who believes has all the spiritual blessings of Eph 1:3-14. The believer will appear faultless before God. Being holy and blameless can either refer to the day the believer will see the Lord (1 John 3:3) or what the believer currently is in Christ. God has accomplished this "in love" when He predestined the believer for this

---

[24] William Hendriksen, *Exposition of Ephesians,* New Testament Commentary (Grand Rapids, MI: Baker Book House, 1967), 75, 78-79, 87.

[25] Ibid., 78.

[26] E. K. Simpson, *The Epistle of Paul to the Ephesians and to the Colossians,* NICNT, ed. F. F. Bruce (Grand Rapids, MI: Eerdmans, 1975), 25-27.

[27] Ibid., 34.

glory. The human mind cannot comprehend or reconcile how God can do this and how man can have free will at the same time.[28]

However, Chafer also sees a present-day emphasis in this passage. The "adoption as sons" in v 5 involves a process. The believer is called to spiritual maturity in this life, as he no longer lives under the Law of Moses. Such a believer can walk in holiness and serve God.[29]

Since Ironside also believes in the freedom of the will, he agrees with Chafer that we cannot understand election. God is not pictured as being cruel to the unbeliever in this passage because there is no mention of His choosing people for damnation. Ironside reasons that this passage points to the future. God chooses people for eternal life; they are made holy and blameless in the eyes of God because of the cross of Christ; God adopts the believer to be His sons by giving the believer His life; and He predestines them for their eternal future "in love."[30]

C. Corporate Election

Thielman takes what can be called a middle of the road position on election in Eph 1:4-5. The emphasis of this election is not God's choosing individuals. Instead, it finds its parallel in the OT with His choosing the Jewish *nation* as His people. Even though individuals are involved, the election in Ephesians deals with the people of God.[31] Believers in Christ become the people of God.

In addition, Thielman believes that the idea of being holy and blameless has a corporate emphasis. God called the nation of Israel to be holy and blameless and an example to other nations of how to live and to show by their actions that they were God's people. Ephesians 1:4 refers to how the Church should live. To do it "in love" also has a corporate emphasis as the ethical injunctions later in Ephesians indicate (Eph 4:1–6:20).[32] Believers are to love one another.

---

[28] Lewis Sperry Chafer, *The Epistle to the Ephesians* (Grand Rapids, MI: Kregel Publications, 1991), 31-36.

[29] Ibid., 37.

[30] H. A. Ironside, *Ephesians* (Neptune, NJ: Loizeaux Brothers, 2000), 24-26.

[31] Frank Thielman, *Ephesians*, Baker Exegetical Commentary on the New Testament (Grand Rapids, MI: Baker Academic, 2010), 48.

[32] Ibid., 49-51.

However, Thielman does not think the election is completely corporate. God chooses the Church, but He chooses individuals to be a part of that Church. This is individual election to eternal life. God chose them before they were born, and they have no freedom of will. Their inheritance (Eph 1:11) is their individual bodily resurrection. He chose them, however, so that His people (the Church) would be separate from the other people in the world.[33]

Best takes an even harder stand on the corporate nature of God's election. He specifically says that God elected the Church. This election focuses on God's purpose. There is an emphasis throughout Ephesians on the unity of Christians as members of the Church. In Ephesians the elect *group* consists of a Body that includes both Jews and Gentiles, not the elected nation of Jews in the OT.[34] Holy and blameless is not what believers are as a result of who they are in Christ or the imputed righteousness of Christ; instead, the phrase refers to Christian living. There is a need in the Church for "moral effort."[35]

Lincoln takes a view similar to that of Best. He says that God's election involves His choosing a people as He did with Israel (Deut 7:6-8; 14:2). In the case of Israel, it was an election that was for the blessing of the nations, as God told Abraham (Gen 12:1ff). Lincoln calls it a *call to service*.[36]

In the case of the Church, election emphasizes the gratitude the people of God should have towards God, not the destiny of individuals. The goal of election also involves a call to service as the Church is called to live in a holy and blameless way. Holiness involves living "in love" in service to others.[37]

Even though Lincoln does see individual election, it is not the emphasis. First of all, the eternal destiny of the individual believer is intimately related to the destiny of the Church. The Church has a purpose, which is to further God's own glory (Eph 1:6). God's glory

---

[33] Ibid., 45.

[34] Ernest Best, *A Critical and Exegetical Commentary on Ephesians* (Edinburgh: T&T Clark, 1998), 119-20.

[35] Ibid., 123. It is interesting, however, that Best does not think "in love" in Eph 1:4 goes with "holy and without blame." Instead, He says that God chose, or elected, the Church in love.

[36] Andrew T. Lincoln, *Ephesians,* Word Biblical Commentary (Dallas, TX: Word Books, 1990), 23.

[37] Ibid., 24.

is the goal of the Church's existence and predestination. In addition, the individual salvation of the believer has not yet been fulfilled. It has only been initiated.[38] This indicates that Lincoln does not believe the election of individual believers in eternity past guaranteed the eternal salvation of every individual God chose. He does not say it, but it seems implied that the purpose of the Church will be fulfilled.

Pinnock sees election in Eph 1:4-5 as corporate and vocational. He strongly rejects the idea that God has chosen certain individuals for eternal life in eternity past and specifically states that God wills the salvation of all nations.[39] The elect at the present time is the Church, but election is functional as it focuses on what the Church does for humanity.

God has chosen a corporate group of people with the goal to save all of mankind. Others will be added to the elect body, but we don't know who will be added to this "eschatological fellowship."[40]

With others, Pinnock sees a parallel with the Jews of the OT. Their election was communal. It is only the corporate that is unconditional. There is an elect body. However, the individual enjoyment of the privileges of being in that body is conditional. That is the way it was with the Jews.[41]

When Pinnock applies this to the Church, he includes eternal salvation in the privileges the elect Church enjoys. Christ will present His elect people to Himself. This is guaranteed. But in order for individuals within the church to be presented to Christ, they must continue in faith and obedience (Col 1:23).[42] In a type of summary statement, Pinnock says that the election in Eph 1:4-5 is both ecclesiological and missiological as the church implores others to become a part of the elect Church.[43]

---

[38] Ibid., 25, 36.

[39] Clark H. Pinnock, "Divine Election as Corporate, Open, and Vocational," in *Perspectives on Election: 5 Views* (Nashville, TN: B & H Academic, 2006), 279-81.

[40] Ibid., 282.

[41] Ibid., 287.

[42] Ibid. 291. Pinnock seems to be saying that eternal life can be lost by the individual.

[43] Ibid., 315.

D. Summary

While many look at Eph 1:4-5 as a proof text for the election, in eternity past, of individuals for eternal life, there are many others who question whether this is Paul's point. Those who question individual predestination ask if God has elected a group of people instead. If that is the case, the election may not be election to eternal life.

To understand what Eph 1:4-5 teaches on the topic of election, the exegete must take into consideration the context, as well as the meaning of the terms "in love" and "holy and without blame." In addition, it would be helpful to consider how Paul in his other writings uses certain words found in Eph 1:4-5.

III. PAUL'S MEANING OF ELECTION IN EPHESIANS 1

As discussed above, even some scholars who believe the election cited in Ephesians 1 involves the choosing of specific individuals to eternal life recognize that the corporate Church is a major theme of the book.

A. Election as Corporate

As noted, Paul uses plural nouns throughout Ephesians 1. He refers to the election of "us" and the election of Jews and Gentiles. The Body of Christ is a major theme. He continues this idea in chap. 2. He says that the Gentiles ("you," plural) were dead in sins (2:1) prior to coming to faith in Christ. The Jews ("we") were in the same situation (2:3).

In Eph 2:11-14, Paul specifically states that God has made both groups, Jews and Gentiles, into one. God has created a "new man," which is the Church. The Church is a household and a building. God dwells within that building (2:19-22).

In Ephesians 3, Paul says that the church was a mystery (3:4); it was not revealed in the OT. In this context, he says that Gentiles are fellow "heirs" with Jewish believers, which reminds the reader of the inheritance of 1:11. All of this was in accordance with God's eternal purposes in Christ. This seems to be a clear reference to the purpose of God in eternity past as discussed in Eph 1:3*ff.*

In Ephesians 4–6, Paul exhorts the believers at Ephesus to use their spiritual gifts to build up the Body of Christ (4:12). These chapters are then filled with how believers are to treat one another as members of that Body.

In Ephesians, Paul never speaks of the individual believer as chosen or predestinated by God. God's election is spoken of in plural terms, and the purpose of God is fulfilled in the Church. The purpose of God is fulfilled when Jewish and Gentile believers love one another and build each other up.

At face value, shouldn't the reader conclude that God has chosen the Church to accomplish His purposes? It would seem that the burden of proof would rest on those who claim Paul is speaking of individual election to eternal life.

B. Holy and Without Blame in Love

While many take the words "holy and without blame" in Eph 1:4 to refer to the believer's position in Christ, there are good reasons to see them as referring to the Christian's manner of life. Outside of Ephesians, Paul only uses the word for "without blame" (*amōmos)* two other times—Phil 2:15 and Col 1:22. In both of these cases Paul is discussing Christian living and a conditional way of life. This is a common way of understanding the word.[44]

The same can be said about the word "holy" (*hagios*). While often in the NT the word is used to refer to believers as "saints" or is used to describe the "Holy" Spirit, it often carries the idea of a person who is reverent or a loyal follower of Christ.[45] Paul uses it in Eph 3:5 to describe the "holy" apostles and prophets. He uses it in 1 Cor 7:34 and Col 1:22 to describe Christian living.

A key point in this discussion is what the phrase "in love" modifies. Hoehner points out that there are three options. It can modify the verb "chose" in v 4. It can modify "predestinated" in v 5. Or it can modify the phrase "holy and without blame." Even though Hoehner takes the position that the election in Ephesians 1 deals with election of individuals to eternal life, he says that "in love" modifies "holy and without blame." It is too far removed from the verb "chose." As

---

[44] BDAG, 56.
[45] Ibid., 11.

a prepositional phrase, "in love" is used in Ephesians five times. Four of those times it follows the clause it modifies (Eph 4:2, 15, 16; 5:2). Here that clause would be "holy and without blame" and not "predestinated." The same is true in other places in Paul's writings (Col 2:2; 1 Thess 5:13; 1 Tim 4:12; 2 Tim 1:13). In Ephesians it is a love that is displayed between humans.[46]

In the ethical section of Ephesians, Paul tells the church at Ephesus to love one another, including the idea that they should walk in love and speak the truth to one another in love (4:2, 15, 16; 5:2). In addition, Paul closes the letter with an exhortation that the church at Ephesus should be at peace with and have love towards one another (6:23). The verb "love" is used in 5:25, 28, 33 to describe how believing married couples should treat one another.[47]

The point here is that in Eph 1:4, "holy and without blame" does not refer to what the individual believer is as a result of his faith in Christ. Instead, it refers to how believers should live. Particularly, it refers to how believers within the church should live in their relationship with each other.

C. Adoption as Sons (1:5) and Inheritance (1:11)

Paul also says that God chose the church for "adoption as sons." In Greek it is only one word (*huiothesian*). While many believe this is a description of all believers, Paul's use here, as well as in other places, suggests otherwise. In Rom 8:15 the word refers to those believers who walk by the Spirit. It refers to an adult, or mature, son.[48] The word is used that way by Paul in Gal 4:5 as well.

Hoehner and Lazar both see this word as referring to more than simply being a believer and child of God. Both point out that the term is associated with the Roman practice of adoption. In that system it

---

[46] Hoehner, *Ephesians*, 182-84.

[47] Lincoln, *Ephesians*, 17.

[48] Zane C. Hodges, *Romans: Deliverance from Wrath* (Corinth, TX: Grace Evangelical Society, 2013), 222. There is a difference in Rom 8:14-16 between being a child of God and a son of God. In Galatians there is a difference between being a child and being a mature son as well.

involved inheriting the estate of the adoptive father. It was the means by which the authority of the father was passed to his adult son.[49]

This fits nicely with the idea of the inheritance mentioned in v 11. The Church has an inheritance from her Father. In Eph 1:18 Paul mentions this inheritance again.[50] In that context Paul says that Christ will be above every power in the age to come. He will rule over all things (vv 21-22). The church is His body and will share in that authority and inheritance with Him.

D. "Before Him" and Colossians 1:22-23

Paul says the purpose of the election of the church is that it would be holy and blameless "before Him" (v 4, *katenōpion autou*). Again, while many take this to mean that believers will appear sinless before Christ on the day of judgment, there is a better alternative based upon the above discussion.

All believers will appear before Christ at the Judgment Seat of Christ. The goal of the election of the Church is that it would appear before God as those who walked in a holy and blameless way by loving one another. Those who have done so will be rewarded on that day. They will receive the inheritance of ruling with Christ in His kingdom.

This is supported by a parallel passage. Colossians 1:22 is the only other place the phrase "before Him" appears. It also has the exact same words "holy and without blame." Many have noted the parallels between Eph 1:4 and Col 1:22.[51] It should be noted, in addition, that both Ephesians and Colossians were written by Paul during the same imprisonment. It would not be surprising if similar ideas were present in both letters.

---

[49] Shawn Lazar, *Chosen to Serve: Why Divine Election Is to Service, Not to Eternal Life* (Denton, TX: Grace Evangelical Society, 2017), 209; Hoehner, *Ephesians,* 186. Hoehner, however, does not see this as related to the issues of rewards, as this article argues.

[50] In v 11 Paul uses the verb and in v 18 the noun.

[51] See, for example Pinnock, "Divine Election," 291; Lincoln, *Ephesians,* 24; Norman L. Geisler, "Colossians," in *The Bible Knowledge Commentary,* New Testament Edition (Wheaton, IL: Victor Books, 1983), 674; and J. B. Bond, "Ephesians," in *The Grace New Testament Commentary,* vol 2 (Denton, TX: Grace Evangelical Society, 2010), 863.

In Col 1:22-23, Paul tells the Colossian believers that they will be presented before Christ holy and without blame only if they continue steadfast in the faith. In Col 1:28, Paul says that his goal is to present them to Christ as mature believers. In this light, the Colossian believers have a "hope of glory."

Since Paul is talking to believers, he cannot be threatening them with the loss of eternal salvation, which is impossible. Instead, Paul is speaking of the day when they will appear before the Judgment Seat of Christ (Rom 14:10; 2 Cor 5:10). On that day, faithful believers will be greatly rewarded and share in the "glory" of reigning with Christ (Col 1:27; Rom 8:17; 2 Tim 2:12). Paul wants the believers at Colossae to stand before Christ on that day with those results.

Clearly, this is conditional for the believers at Colossae and for individual Christians. Paul says he teaches them so that this will happen. They must continue in the faith and not be influenced by the false teachers at Colossae (Col 1:23, 28).[52]

This fits nicely with Ephesians 1. The Church has a glorious inheritance. It will rule with Christ in the world to come. God chose the Church to walk in holiness while loving one another. All believers who do so and remain faithful to the Lord will reign with Him. They will be the ones declared mature sons when they stand before the Lord. While Christ and the Church corporate will rule, not every believer will.

---

[52] Many commentators recognize that this is conditional even though they mistakenly apply it to eternal salvation and not rewards. See, J. B. Lightfoot, *Saint Paul's Epistles to the Colossians and to Philemon* (Grand Rapids, MI: Zondervan, 1976), 163; Herbert M. Carson, *The Epistles of Paul to the Colossians and Philemon* (Grand Rapids, MI: Eerdmans, 1984), 48; David W. Pao, *Colossians and Philemon* (Grand Rapids, MI: Zondervan, 2012), 109; Peter T. O'Brien, *Colossians, Philemon*, Word Biblical Commentary (Nashville, TN: Thomas Nelson, 2000), 68-72.

IV. CONCLUSION

In Eph 1:4-5, Paul says that God predestinated the Church in eternity past. He did so in order that it would walk in good works (Eph 2:10). As the Body of Christ, the Church has a glorious future, an eternal inheritance in the kingdom of God. It will rule that kingdom with the Lord (Eph 1:11, 18-23).

When God chose the nation of Israel in the OT for a purpose, not every individual in the nation achieved that purpose. They were called to be a light to other nations. They were called to serve. They had a job to do. The same is true in the Church.[53]

Only those believers who are faithful to the Lord (Col 1:23) do the works God requires of them. They live holy and blameless lives and will be found that way at the Judgment Seat of Christ. While all believers will be in the kingdom, only those who are found this way on that day will be the mature sons who receive the inheritance of their Father.

Believers are not chosen individually for eternal life. Unbelievers have the freedom to believe the gospel. Believers are only chosen "in Christ" and are part of the Church.[54] As members of the Church we are called to serve those in the Church in love.

---

[53] Lazar, *Chosen to Serve*, 207; See also, C. Gordon Olson, *Beyond Calvinism and Arminianism: An Inductive Mediate Theology of Salvation*, 3rd ed. (Lynchburg, VA: Global Gospel Publishers, 2002), 336.

[54] Lazar, *Chosen to Serve*, 205.

THE PRACTICAL SYLLOGISM AND ASSURANCE

ROBERT N. WILKIN

Associate Editor

I. INTRODUCTION

The English branch of the Reformation developed a view of assurance that relied significantly on what became known as *the practical syllogism*. Since the Puritans considered regeneration to be unknowable by purely objective means, they sought for indirect ways to determine whether one was regenerate.[1] Most Puritans believed that there were two indirect (i.e., subjective) means: *the practical syllogism* (focus on external actions) and *the mystical syllogism* (focus on the inner person, especially godly inclinations).[2] This paper will consider only the practical syllogism.

It is the thesis of this paper that the works-based practical syllogism produces doubt, not assurance.

II. THE PURITAN USE OF THE PRACTICAL SYLLOGISM

Puritan theologians use the practical syllogism in order to provide Calvinists with knowledge of their regenerate status, as well as motivation for wholehearted service for God.

Joel Beeke wrote his dissertation at Westminster Theological Seminary on "Personal Assurance of Faith: English Puritanism and the Dutch Nadere Reformatie from Westminster to Alexander Comrie (1640-1760)." His book *The Quest for Full Assurance* is a

---

[1] Also uncertain is whether Christ died for you, whether God has drawn you, and whether you will persevere in faith and good works until the end of life. The practical syllogism is designed to help answer all those questions affirmatively.

[2] The mystical syllogism looks not at external works and transformation, but at inward grace and godliness. The mystical syllogism focuses on inner attitudes and feelings, rather than observable actions.

revision of his dissertation.[3] Beeke explains the practical syllogism in this way:

> The practical syllogism was based on the believer's sanctification and good works in daily life. It emphasized the believer's life of obedience that confirmed his experience of grace. It went something like this: *Major premise:* According to Scripture, only those who possess saving faith will receive the Spirit's testimony that their lives manifest fruits of sanctification and good works. *Minor premise:* I cannot deny that by the grace of God I have received the Spirit's testimony that I manifest fruits of sanctification and good works. *Conclusion:* I am a partaker of saving faith.[4]

The major premise concerns something which is true of believers. The minor premise is what is true of me as an individual. The conclusion is that I am a believer. Here is a simplified version of the assurance syllogism:

Major Premise:	Believers[5] manifest good works.
Minor Premise:	I manifest good works.
Conclusion:	I am a believer.[6]

The focus in the practical syllogism is external and subjective (i.e., good works, sanctification, transformation, perseverance). The aim is to provide a way in which to verify that the cross and the promise of everlasting life apply to you.

III. EVIDENCE THAT THE PURITAN PRACTICAL SYLLOGISM IS INCONSISTENT WITH SCRIPTURE

The Puritans were seeking to glorify God via the practical syllogism. However, the Scriptures do not support the practical syllogism.

---

[3] Joel R. Beeke, *The Quest for Full Assurance* (Carlisle, PA: The Banner of Truth Trust, 1999), vii.

[4] Ibid., 132.

[5] Following Beeke, I refer to believers in the major premise. However, I could also refer to born again people or to the elect.

[6] This is Beeke's explanation of the syllogism, simplified.

A. Born Again People Who Failed to Persevere in Good Works

1 Corinthians 11:30. The believers at Corinth were guilty of partaking in the Lord's Supper in an unworthy manner. Some of them were getting drunk and overeating. As a result, Paul said, "Some of you are sick and some sleep." The word "sleep" (*koimaō*) in all other NT uses, when it is used figuratively of death, always refers to the death *of believers* (John 11:11, 12, 13; 1 Thess 4:14). This includes the one other use in 1 Corinthians (15:51). Though these believers had been guilty of misbehavior at the Lord's Supper and had died prematurely as a result, they still went to be with the Lord.

2 Timothy 4:10. Demas was listed in Colossians and Philemon as one of Paul's trusted co-workers (Col 4:14; Phlm 1:24). In Philippians, another of the prison epistles, Paul had said:

> I implore Euodia and I implore Syntyche to be of the same mind in the Lord. And I urge you also, true companion, help these women who labored with me in the gospel, with Clement also, and the rest of my fellow workers, whose names are in the Book of Life (Phil 4:2-3).

Since Demas was one of Paul's fellow workers, his name was and remains in the Book of Life.

Yet years later as Paul faces death by martyrdom after his second Roman imprisonment, he writes concerning Demas, "Be diligent to come to me quickly; for Demas has forsaken me, having loved this present world, and has departed for Thessalonica..." (2 Tim 4:9-10).

This is the last we hear of Demas: "Demas has forsaken me, having loved this present world." Whether he, like John Mark, later returned to ministry and to loving the world to come is not stated. Yet Paul does not question his regenerate status. Paul finds fault with the behavior of Demas, not his eternal destiny.

B. Born Again People Who Failed to Rise Beyond Baby Christian Status

The practical syllogism requires that believers steadily progress. For someone to be stalled in immaturity would suggest that he was not born again.

The believers in Corinth had been in Christ for about five years when Paul composed 1 Corinthians. He writes to them:

> And I, brethren, could not speak to you as to spiritual people but as to carnal, as to babes in Christ. I fed you with milk and not with solid food; for until now you were not able to receive it, and even now you are still not able; for you are still carnal. For where there are envy, strife, and divisions among you, are you not carnal, and behaving like mere men? (1 Cor 3:1-3).

The problem for the practical syllogism is that Paul does call the Corinthians *natural men*, or *mere men*. He calls them "babes in Christ." He affirms that they were *in Christ*. All who are "in Christ" in the Pauline sense have everlasting life.

In verse 3 the first word in Greek is *still* (*eti*): "Still you are now not able…"

I suppose one could argue that they later all achieved the status of mature believers or spiritual people. But there is no hint of that in the rest of 1 Corinthians or in 2 Corinthians or in any of Paul's other letters. Besides, those who died for abusing the Lord's Supper clearly never reached maturity (1 Cor 11:30).

C. Promises of Everlasting Life Specifically Detached from Works

If all who have everlasting life will persevere in good works, then we must not see passages which deny any necessary connection between the two. Yet when asked, "What shall we do, that we may work the works of God?" (John 6:28), the Lord Jesus answered, "This is the work of God, that you believe in Him whom He sent" (John 6:29).

They spoke of "works," plural. He spoke of one "work," using the word *work* ironically. The only action a person can do to gain everlasting life is to believe in God's Son, the Lord Jesus Christ.

If good works necessarily follow faith in Christ, then the Lord would have said something different. He would have said something like, "The works of God are to believe in Him whom He sent and then to love Him and your neighbor throughout your lives."

See also Eph 2:8-9. Salvation, which is being made alive by God (Eph 2:5), is by grace through faith and apart from works. And it is something which is an accomplished and irreversible event: "you have been saved." The perfect passive speaks of something which God did in the past to them and which has an abiding result.[7]

D. Rebuke by Christ of People Seeking Assurance in Their Works

The Lord Jesus rebuked legalistic Jews in His day when He said, "You search the Scriptures, for in them you think you have eternal life; and these are they which testify of Me. But you are not willing to come to Me that you may have life" (John 5:39-40).

The legalists were looking to the commands of Scripture for assurance that they were good enough to enter the coming kingdom.

Searching the Scriptures can be a good thing. The only other reference to this idea is very positive (Acts 17:11). But here in John 5:39-40, it was not good because the purpose of the searching was wrong. Rather than trying to learn what God said one must do to have everlasting life, the legalists were searching the OT to find evidence in their works that they had eternal life.

But, the Lord says the Scriptures testify about Messiah. If the listeners had come to the OT and to Jesus with open minds and hearts, they would have gained everlasting life by faith apart from works.

See also the end of the Sermon on the Mount in which the Lord specifically rebukes those who think they will get into His kingdom because of works they have done in His name (Matt 7:21-23). Works are not the basis of assurance. Faith in Christ is.

E. The Gospel of Belief

John's Gospel is called *the Gospel of Belief* because the word *believe* (*pisteuō*) occurs 99 times (100 in the Majority Text). Over and over again belief is said to be the sole condition for everlasting life (e.g., John 1:11-13; 3:14-18, 36; 4:10-14; 5:24, 39-40; 6:35, 37, 39, 47; 11:25-27; 20:30-31).

---

[7] Verse 10 does not support the idea of guaranteed perseverance, either. Most fail to notice the shift from the second person plural in Eph 2:8-9 to the first person plural in Eph 2:10 (and following). Verse 10 is corporate. The Church of Jesus Christ, made up of Jews and Gentiles undivided (Eph 2:11*ff.*) is God's workmanship. The Church should produce manifestly good works. Of course, we know from the two letters to the Corinthians and the seven letters to the seven churches in Revelation 2-3 that not all churches are characterized by good works.

Not only is belief the condition of everlasting life, it is also the basis of assurance of it, according to the Lord in John's Gospel. That makes sense, of course, since *believing* and *being assured* are synonyms. When you are assured of something, you believe it. When you believe something, you are assured it is true.

The Puritan practical syllogism is inconsistent with God's Word.

IV. THE LOGICAL PROBLEM WITH THE PURITAN PRACTICAL SYLLOGISM

The Puritan practical syllogism is guilty of *affirming the consequent.* Shawn Lazar says, "Let's assume that saved people do good works and that you do good works. However, being saved [the conclusion of the practical syllogism] is not the only explanation for why you might do good works."[8]

He goes on to suggest that Buddhists, Muslims, and Jehovah's Witnesses all do good works too. Protestants and Catholics who believe in works-salvation do good works. Politicians, people seeking scholarships, and guys who want to win girls all do good works. He concludes, "Being saved is only one possible explanation among many for doing good works. Hence the conclusion does not necessarily follow from the premises. It is invalid."

If you base your assurance in part on looking at your works, then Lazar's point is well taken. Unless your works are absolutely perfect, you have no valid way of setting your works above the works of people who do not claim to be Evangelical Christians. Your works might only prove that you are what seventeenth-century Puritan Matthew Mead called *the almost Christian.*

---

[8] Shawn Lazar, "Assurance and the Fallacy of Affirming the Consequent," *Grace in Focus Magazine*, Nov-Dec 2017, 40.

V. WHY SOME REFORMED THEOLOGIANS QUESTION THE PURITAN PRACTICAL SYLLOGISM

A. It Produces Doubt, Which Is Bad

Beeke argues against assurance by faith alone (e.g., pp. 281, 283, 284). He follows the Westminster Confession, suggesting that assurance comes from "objective promises, subjective sanctification, and internal testimony" (p. 283). Since sanctification and the so-called inner testimony of the Spirit are both subjective, Beeke concludes that "faith will bear varying degrees of assurance" (p. 285).

Whatever *assurance* is for Beeke, it cannot be certainty, for there are no degrees of certainty.

Yet Beeke recognizes a practical problem with the practical syllogism. When discussing the Puritan practical syllogism, Beeke issues a warning about a potential danger in self-examination:

> If introspective probing of the realm of private experience takes precedence over seeking communion with God in Christ, the resulting imbalance will bring more darkness than light. Divorced from God's promises, the reflex act would be more disheartening than assuring, *for the Christian often discovers in self-examination that he is either missing many of the marks of grace or else finds them so defective that he would despair if faith did not rest on God's Word.*[9]

Beeke's point seems to be that assurance is found primarily in believing God's promises plus, in part, on seeing some works which, while imperfect, give a bit of subjective evidence to add to the objective promises.

Warnings about being *too introspective* are given by many Calvinists.

In Appendix E of the revised edition of *The Five Points of Calvinism* by Steele, Thomas, and Quinn, Curt Daniel warns:

> Another odd pitfall that characterizes some Calvinists is chronic introspection. Now I do not mean normal self-inspection (2 Cor. 13:5). I mean the sort that goes too far. This sort seems to glory in introspection without the proper results. What do I mean? True self-examination should lead to renewed faith and love and obedience. False introspection leads to more introspection and

---

[9] Beeke, *The Quest for Full Assurance*, 139, emphases added.

actually less faith. It produces more doubt, not faith. For example, some worry that they might not be among the elect…[10]

Michael Eaton says that introspection is:

…the snag of scholastic Calvinism. It leads into an abyss of ever-increasing introspection…The more sincere the Christian, the more severe the doubts…There are subtle variations among different versions of Calvinism. The introspective variety is decidedly not totally derived from the New Testament, and its all-pervasive view of the law needs reconsidering.[11]

Retired professor David Engelsma, also a Calvinist, gives a stronger warning. He believes that introspection is bad, no matter how carefully one does it:

Do not quench the Spirit of assurance either by listening to Puritan preaching that is forever questioning your assurance, forever challenging your right to assurance, forever sending you on a quest for assurance, and forever instilling doubt. The Spirit does not work assurance by means of a gospel of doubt.[12]

Seventeenth-century Puritan Matthew Mead (1629-1699) wrote a book entitled *The Almost Christian Discovered*. It was recently republished with a foreword from John MacArthur.[13] The many warnings he gives show the dangers of introspection.

Mead goes to great lengths to strip any Puritan of false confidence that he is born again. See Appendix 2 in this article for a list of all twenty of the warnings he gives. Mead says that the following may be true of you and yet you may still be an almost Christian: you may have "spiritual gifts" (warning 2); "great hopes of heaven" (warning 9); "the Spirit of God" (warning 15); and "faith" (warning 16). In addition, he says you may "hate sin" (warning 5), "be under great

---

[10] Cited in David N. Steele, Curtis C. Thomas, and S. Lance Quinn, *The Five Points of Calvinism*, 2nd ed. (Phillipsburg, NJ: P & R Publishing, 1963, 2004), 195. Appendix E is from Curt Daniel's book *The History and Theology of Calvinism* (Dallas, TX: Scholarly Reprints, 1983), 465-70.

[11] Michael A. Eaton, *No Condemnation: A Theology of Assurance of Salvation* (Carlisle, UK: Piquant Editions, 2011), 36.

[12] David Engelsma, *The Gift of Assurance* (The Evangelism Committee of the Protestant Reformed Church: South Holland, IL: 2009), 53.

[13] Matthew Mead, *The Almost Christian Discovered* (Ligonier, PA: Soli Deo Gloria Publications, first printed in 1661, SDGP reprint 1989).

and visible changes, and these wrought by the ministry of the word" (warning 10), "pray often, and pray much" (warning 12), "suffer for Christ" (warning 13), "obey many of the commands of God" (warning 18), and "be sanctified" (warning 19).

In the foreword to *The Almost Christian Discovered*, MacArthur says, "Self-examination is thoroughly biblical (2 Corinthians 13:5)... That is exactly what this book is all about. Don't read it unless you are willing to undergo the most intense kind of personal inventory."[14]

The concern of Beeke, Daniel, Eaton, and Engelsma seems justified in light of the lengths Mead and other Puritans go to strip assurance from those who call themselves Christians.

B. It Is Not Found in Scripture

Zachman, Engelsma, Kendall, and Eaton all suggest that the Scriptures do not support the idea that assurance is based in part on the objective promises of Scripture and in part on our works and feelings. They cite John 3:16 and other texts as teaching that assurance is based *solely on the objective promises* found in God's Word. The promise of everlasting life is to everyone who believes, not to those who believe plus work, plus feel an inner testimony.[15]

Concerning 2 Cor 13:5-7, Kendall writes:

> Paul is not turning on them at the last moment and raising the question whether or not they are even saved...He challenges them to prove their own worth in the light of his apostleship being questioned. The Greek does not read, "Examine yourselves *to see* if you are in the faith"; it is rather, "Examine yourselves if you *are in the faith*." As they were seeking a proof of Christ speaking through Paul (2 Cor. 13:3), Paul turns on them and asks them to prove that Christ is speaking through them!...The contrast is not that of being saved or lost but whether, as saved people, Christ is openly manifest in them.[16]

---

[14] Ibid., 1.

[15] See, for example, R. T. Kendall, *Once Saved, Always Saved* (London: Hodder and Stoughton, 1983), 19-21.

[16] Ibid., 130, emphases his.

C. It Undercuts Careful Hermeneutics

If I read the Bible in such a way that I cannot be sure I have everlasting life, this impacts the way I understand everything from Genesis to Revelation. If I adopt a hermeneutic that sees John 3:16 as a tough text, then I will see much of the Bible as tough texts.

VI. A FAITH-ONLY PRACTICAL SYLLOGISM

There is another type of practical syllogism that relies not upon on works or our feelings, but upon what we believe:

Major Premise:	If you believe in Jesus for everlasting life you are regenerate.
Minor Premise:	I believe in Jesus for everlasting life.
Conclusion:	I am regenerate.

If believing God's promise of everlasting life is objective, as the Westminster Confession suggests (though many modern Calvinists suggest that saving faith has subjective elements such as repentance, surrender, commitment, and personal encounter with Christ), then under this syllogism one could be sure that one is born again.

Though they do not call it *a practical syllogism*, a number of Calvinists (or former Calvinists) use this syllogism, including David Engelsma, Randall Zachman, R. T. Kendall, and Michael Eaton. For example, discussing Calvin's view of assurance, Zachman says, "The foundation of our assurance lies not in what God is doing within us by the gift of regeneration, but rather in the promise of what God freely gives us in Christ Jesus."[17] He then adds, "Doubt and uncertainty cannot help but arise when we bring our works into consideration to found our assurance."[18]

---

[17] Randall C. Zachman, *The Assurance of Faith: Conscience in the Theology of Martin Luther and John Calvin* (Minneapolis, MN: Fortress Press, 1993), 210.

[18] Ibid. Zachman continues, "Therefore, even though Calvin is at pains to show that faith in justification is never found apart from repentance and newness of life, he is equally at pains to establish the foundation of the assurance of conscience in justification alone, for it is only by faith in the reconciling death of Christ that 'we may have in heaven instead of a judge a gracious Father' (Calvin's *Institutes* III. xi.1)."

VII. PRACTICAL APPLICATION

A. Personal Assurance

The Puritan works-based practical syllogism produces doubt, not assurance.

If I look to Christ alone for my assurance, I will be sure. Jesus guarantees everlasting life to all who believe in Him for that life. I believe in Jesus for everlasting life. Therefore, I have everlasting life.

B. Personal Motivations for Serving God

Though Calvinists honor the sovereignty and glory of God, their motivation in serving God is also influenced by the practical syllogism. Calvinists who look to their works for assurance are serving God in part so that they might spend eternity with the Lord.

If our works are needed to gain what some call *final salvation,* then our motivation to do those works is certainly in part a desire to gain that final salvation.

Look to Christ alone for your assurance and you will fall more in love with Him. Love for Him is the single most important motivation there is for serving God.[19]

C. Personal Staying Power

In our day and age, serving Christ faithfully is tough. There are so many challenges trying to distract us and to get us to quit the race. Public education is against us. The media, television, books, and movies are all contrary to following Christ. Advertising also opposes fidelity to Christ.

If we know we have everlasting life that can never be lost, we have a powerful internal motivator to keep us going.

Through the ministry of Campus Crusade for Christ, I came to faith in Christ while I was a senior in college. I had been in a sinless perfection holiness cult until that point. When I heard the

---

[19] Other motivations include a desire for God's blessings now and in the life to come (Leviticus 26; Deuteronomy 28; Luke 19:16-26; 1 Cor 3:10-15; 9:24-27; 2 Cor 5:9-10), a desire to escape temporal judgment in this life (Leviticus 26; Deuteronomy 28; Jas 5:19-20), and a desire to make one's life count, to have a life that has eternal significance (Matt 6:1-21).

faith-alone message, I rejected it as cheap and easy and a trick of the devil. But since a friend from the cult challenged me to consider this grace message, I went to a College Life meeting with him. Later I met with Warren Wilke, a staff member, for five weeks, an hour a week. Warren was like a broken record, quoting Eph 2:8-9. Finally after five weeks I believed. I was sure I had been saved once and for all by grace, through faith, and apart from works.

The cult had said if you had such assurance you would go to the dogs, meaning you would drink and do drugs and cuss and smoke and commit immorality. I found that assurance of everlasting life had the opposite impact. Within a few months, I was sharing my faith regularly on campus. I wanted to serve God. I changed from pre-med to pre-ministry at the start of my senior year in college.

I have been serving Christ for 46 years now. I have found that assurance by faith keeps me going.

In the summer of 1982, after I graduated from DTS, I asked Dr. Charles Ryrie if he would conduct my ordination council and preach my ordination sermon. He agreed. Then he said, "The key, Bob, is whether you will still be faithfully proclaiming God's Word 40 years from now."

It has been 36 years since Dr. Ryrie said that and his words still ring in my head. It all starts with believing God's promise of everlasting life.

D. Personal Evangelism

How do you share your faith with others? Surely you tell them what you believe the Bible says.

If you believe the Bible says that those who persevere in faith and good works will gain final salvation, then that is the message you will proclaim. But that is not the saving message which our Lord proclaimed.

To clearly evangelize others, tell them about the promise of life to all who simply believe in Jesus.

Some Calvinists speak of evangelizing themselves as personal evangelism. They remind themselves of the need to persevere. But that is wrong. We should remind ourselves that we believe in Jesus and that all who believe in Jesus have everlasting life. That is powerful.

VIII. CONCLUSION

There is no doubt that assurance of everlasting life is an important Biblical doctrine and that it has tremendous practical benefit for the believer. The practical syllogism, while well-intentioned, fails to deliver assurance of everlasting life.

At best, the syllogism can lead one to conclude that he is *probably* born again. But to achieve even this sub-assurance level of probability, one must take care not to put much stock in introspection.

One can only be certain that he has everlasting life if he looks outside himself to the promise of the Lord Jesus that the one who believes in Him has everlasting life and shall never hunger, never thirst, never perish, never die, and never come into judgment concerning his eternal destiny (John 3:16; 5:24; 6:35, 47; 11:25-26).

The Lord Jesus Christ is the Truth, as well as the Way and the Life. We can be certain that whoever believes in Him has everlasting life.

In a chapter on "Perseverance and Assurance" in his systematic theology, Calvinist John Frame cites two verses in the Fourth Gospel to prove that "Clearly, God promises eternal life to all who receive Christ (John 1:12…6:35…)."[20] He goes on to say that while his name is not listed in the Bible explicitly, "my name is there *implicitly*."[21] He went on to say that, "God promises salvation to everybody who believes. If you believe, then, that promise is yours. God promises to save you. And that promise is infallible, certain. You dare not doubt it."[22]

---

[20] John M. Frame, *Systematic Theology: An Introduction to Christian Belief* (Phillipsburg, NJ: P & R Publishing, 2013), 1004.

[21] Ibid, 1005, emphasis his.

[22] Ibid.

APPENDIX 1: THE ORIGIN OF THE PRACTICAL SYLLOGISM

The generic practical syllogism goes back to Greek philosophy. Aristotle (384-322 BC) said that a major premise states some universal truth, a minor premise states a particular truth, and the conclusion is an action which should result.[23]

Here is an example slightly modified from Wikipedia's discussion of the practical syllogism in Aristotle's treatise on ethics called the *Nicomachean Ethics*:

Major premise:	All men should exercise (universal).
Minor premise:	I am a man (particular).
Conclusion:	I should exercise (a reasonable action).[24]

In a practical syllogism the conclusion can be an action to be taken, knowledge to be believed, or motivation for future action.

APPENDIX 2: *THE ALMOST CHRISTIAN DISCOVERED*

As mentioned earlier, Matthew Mead of the seventeenth century gave twenty warnings about the possibility of being what he called "an almost Christian." Those twenty warnings are:

1. "A man may have much knowledge, and yet be but almost a Christian."

2. "A man may have great and eminent gifts, yea, spiritual gifts, and yet be but almost a Christian."

3. "A man may have a high profession of religion, be much in external duties of godliness, and yet be but almost a Christian."

4. "A man may go far in opposing his sin, and yet be but almost a Christian."

5. "A man may hate sin, and yet be but almost a Christian."

---

[23] See *DeAnima* 434a 15-20. See also Alexander Broadie, "The Practical Syllogism," *Analysis* (October 1968): 26-28.

[24] Wikipedia, s.v., "Practical Syllogism."

6. "A man may make great vows and promises, he may have strong purposes and resolutions against sin, and yet be but almost a Christian."

7. "A man may maintain a strife and combat against sin in himself, and yet be but almost a Christian."

8. "A man may be a member of the Church of Christ, he may join himself to the people of God, partake with them in all ordinances, and share of all church privileges, and yet be but almost a Christian."

9. "A man may have great hopes of heaven, great hopes of being saved, and yet be but almost a Christian."

10. "A man may be under great and visible changes, and these wrought by the ministry of the word, and yet be but almost a Christian."

11. "A man may be very zealous in the matters of religion, and yet be but almost a Christian."

12. "A man may be much in prayer—he may pray often, and pray much, and yet be but almost a Christian."

13. "A man may suffer for Christ in his goods, in his name, in his person, and yet be but almost a Christian."

14. "A man may be called of God, and embrace this call, and be but almost a Christian."

15. "A man may have the Spirit of God, and yet be but almost a Christian."

16. "A man may have faith, and yet be but almost a Christian."

17. "A man may have a love to the people of God, and yet be but almost a Christian."

18. "A man may obey the commands of God, yea, many of the commands of God, and yet be but almost a Christian."

19. "A man may be sanctified, and yet be but almost a Christian."

20. "A man may do all, as to external duties and worship, that a true Christian can, and when he hath done all, be but almost a Christian."[25]

So what is Mead's solution? First, use self-examination (pp. 164-175). Look to see if you have a new heart and a new spirit (p. 165).

---

[25] Mead, *The Almost Christian Discovered*, 3-7 in the Table of Contents, and at the heading of each of these sections, pp. 40, 43, 48, 55, 63, 66, 69, 76, 78, 81, 85, 92, 96, 98, 100, 103, 108, 112, 116, 119, respectively.

"Regeneration is a whole change: 'old things are done away, and all things become new. It is a perfect work, as to parts, though not as to degrees'" (p. 170). "Is thy obedience universal?" (p. 175). Second, use caution (pp. 175-189). That is, "take heed of being almost, and yet but almost a Christian" (p. 175). The Puritan never can escape the need to doubt his own eternal destiny. Third, use exhortation (pp. 189-211). Here Mead speaks of "motives to quicken you up to this important duty" (p. 189). As if the motive of avoiding eternity in the lake of fire would not be enough, Mead speaks of various motivations bound up in the exhortations of Scripture, like following Christ is profitable for us and produces comfort and relief in us.

APPENDIX 3: ANANIAS AND SAPPHIRA (ACTS 5:1-11)

Ananias and his wife Sapphira are the NT counterparts to Nadab and Abihu in the OT.

When the Law of Moses was being inaugurated, Aaron's two oldest sons offered up strange fire on their firepans and were struck dead by God on the spot (Lev 10:1-7). Right after this, the Lord gave Aaron instructions that the priests were not to drink wine or intoxicating drink "when you go into the tabernacle of meeting, lest you die" (Lev 10:8-9). The implication is that Nadab and Abihu were drunk when they were burned with fire from heaven.

Shortly after God inaugurated the church age, another couple, this time husband and wife, were also struck dead by God. They sold land, kept back some of the proceeds of the sale, and then told the Apostles that they were giving the entire proceeds from the sale. Both lied. Because the issue here, as in Leviticus 10, was the holiness of God, He struck them both dead.

Ananias and Sapphira were born again people. Peter did not evangelize them. He exercised church discipline. The concluding verse shows that the other believers present realized this could happen to them as well: "So great fear came upon all the church and upon all who heard these things" (Acts 5:11).

THE STONE/ROCK/TOMB
MOTIF IN MATTHEW

BOB SWIFT

In Memoriam[1]

I. INTRODUCTION

In Matthew's Gospel, the words "stone" (*lithos*) and "rock" (*petra*) occur ten times (Matt 3:9; 4:3, 6; 7:9; 21:42, 44; 24:2; 27:60, 66; 28:2) and five times (Matt 7:24, 25; 16:18; 27:51, 60),[2] respectively. The related word "tomb" (*taphos* or *mnēmeion*) occurs thirteen times (*taphos* in Matt 23:27, 29; 27:61, 64, 66; 28:1; *mnēmeion* in Matt 8:28; 23:29; 27:52, 53, 60 [2x]; 28:8).

As I reflected on the raised saints in Matt 27:51-54, it struck me that the rock/stone/tomb motif is a vital one, not only for that passage, but for all of Matthew's Gospel. In the Matthew 27 passage we see rocks split and the tombs of certain dead believers opened, accompanied by their bodily resurrection. This results in the confession of the centurion concerning Christ, that He is the Son of God, in Matt 27:54. In Matt 16:18 we see that Peter's great confession of Jesus as the Christ, the Son of God, is the "rock" upon which Jesus would build His church.

---

[1] Editor's note: Bob Swift was a long time friend of the Grace Evangelical Society. He was an avid student of the Word of God. On March 18, 2018, Bob went to be with the Lord after a long illness. In the past, he had written articles for this journal. This article was the last one he sent to GES, just a few months prior to his departure. It is published in memory of Bob. Except for a few editor footnotes and format changes, the article is as Bob wrote it.

[2] Mark has the word *petra* only once, while Luke has five uses. Mark has eight uses of *lithos*, and Luke has fourteen uses. While this motif can be seen in all of the Synoptics, I have focused on Matthew because it seems to be more prevalent there.

Could it be mere coincidence that both confessions are linked with rocks? It seems to me that the Holy Spirit produced the miracle of the split rocks and moved Matthew to include this account (not found in the other Gospels) to highlight the confessions of both the centurion and Peter.

But just as the rocks were split and the tombs of OT saints were opened, Jesus' own tomb was later sealed with a stone. His grave was opened as well, as the stone was rolled away.

II. STONE/ROCK/TOMB PLAY A PROMINENT ROLE, ESPECIALLY LATER IN THE GOSPEL

References to stones or rocks in Matthew are not found uniformly throughout the book. Instead, the references occur at the start of Jesus' ministry (Matthew 3, 4, 7) and at the end (Matthew 16, 21, 24, 27, 28).

These words are intimately connected with Jesus' temptations, His death, His burial, and His resurrection. Opposition to Jesus and His rejection by the nation are major themes in these chapters. Not surprisingly, in Matthew Jesus refers to Himself as "the *stone* which the builders rejected" (Matt 21:42).[3]

There is only one reference to tombs in the early ministry of Jesus. It involves the two demoniacs who came out of the tombs. Jesus cast the demons out of them (Matt 8:28). All other references to tombs occur after the triumphal entry during the last week of Jesus' ministry and after His death and resurrection.

III. PETER'S CONFESSION IS THE ROCK (MATTHEW 16:18)

When the Lord asks the disciples who they think He is (Matt 16:15), Peter confesses that He is the Christ, the Son of God. After Peter's great confession, Jesus says, "And I also say to you that you are Peter (*petros*) and on this rock (*petra*) I will build my church and the gates of Hades shall not prevail against it." Some think that the Lord

---

[3] We know from Paul in 1 Cor 10:4 that Jesus is also called the Rock which followed Israel in the wilderness wanderings.

was promising to build the church on Peter himself. Yet that fails to consider what Peter has just stated in his great confession. It is Peter's confession of Jesus as the Christ, the Son of God, which is the rock upon which Jesus would build His church. We also see echoes of Peter's confession in Matt 27:54 in the confession of the centurion.

IV. THE CENTURION'S CONFESSION RESULTING FROM THE SPLIT ROCKS AND TOMBS WHICH WERE OPENED (MATTHEW 27:51-54)

Peter's confession in Matt 16:16 is, "You are the Christ, the Son of the living God." Actually, in Greek the confession is more literally, "You are the Christ, the Son of God, the living One" (*ho Huios tou Theou tou zōntos*).

As noted above, following Peter's great confession, Jesus calls him *Petros* and says that upon this *petra* He would build His church.

In Matthew there are only three other confessions of Jesus as the Son of God. One is by Peter and the other disciples when Jesus (and Peter) walked on water, and Jesus calmed a storm (Matt 14:33). Another confession is by the two demon possessed men coming out of the tombs (Matt 8:29). The final one is by the centurion (Matt 27:54).

Even the confession of the demons in Matthew 8 is tied to the rock/stone motif since the men they possessed "came out of the tombs." In light of Jesus' later explanation of why He changed Simon's name to Peter, or *Petros*, in Matt 16:18, the confession in Matthew 14 is also linked to the rock motif since Peter is named as one of those making that confession in the boat.

V. JESUS' BURIAL AND RESURRECTION ARE TIED TO ROCK, STONE, AND TOMB

Although Matthew does not specify this, Jesus' tomb was cut out of rock (Mark 15:46). Matthew does tell us that a stone was placed over the entrance to Jesus' tomb, and it was sealed by the Romans (Matt 27:66). On the Sunday morning of Christ's resurrection, Matthew tells us, "an angel of the Lord descended from heaven, and came and rolled back the stone from the door, and sat on it" (Matt 28:2).

Jesus' death, burial, and resurrection are all linked in Matthew to the rock/stone motif.

In fact, in Matthew 16, after Peter makes his great confession, the Lord went on to tell him and the other disciples that He was going to be killed in Jerusalem and that He would rise from the dead on the third day (Matt 16:21). Peter's response was the polar opposite of his great confession. He went on to rebuke Jesus and to say, "This shall not happen to You!" (Matt 16:22).

Peter and the disciples did not yet understand that the Messiah had to die and rise again. They were thinking in terms of glory now. They expected to rule with Christ without any suffering first.

The man called *Petros* had to learn the full significance of the name the Lord had given to him.

So too did all of His followers. On the third day a group of women came "to see the tomb" (28:1). They came to anoint the body (Mark 16:1). They clearly did not believe that He was going to rise from the dead. None of His followers understood, until after He arose and an angel announced that He had risen, that He would rise from the dead on the third day. Even then, many did not believe until they personally saw Him in His post-resurrection body.

The empty tomb plays a key role in the rock, stone, and tomb motif in Matthew and in Mark and Luke as well. The motif is key to proclaiming who Jesus Christ is.

VI. BUILDING YOUR HOUSE ON THE ROCK (MATTHEW 7:24-28)

Two of the early uses of *petra* in Matthew are found at the end of the Sermon on the Mount (Matthew 7). A life that is built on belief in the teachings of Jesus is like a house that is built "on the rock" (Matt 7:24). Such a life is one that will withstand all that can come against it, as illustrated by rain, floods, and winds.[4]

---

[4] Editor's note: Clearly, this verse has nothing to do with gaining eternal life. As Bob correctly points out, building one's house upon the rock involves living one's life on Christ's teaching. It involves works of obedience. Such a life survives all that may come against it and will result in eternal rewards.

But a life that does not believe and apply Jesus' teachings is one that cannot withstand life's storms. When the wind, rain, and floods come, the person will fall like a house built on sand.

This same motif is picked up later in the Gospel when Matthew cites the Psalmist who spoke of the stone which the builders rejected.

VII. JESUS IS THE STONE WHICH THE BUILDERS REJECTED (MATTHEW 21:42)

In a confrontation with the religious leaders of His day, the Lord Jesus quotes from Ps 118:22-23 concerning "the stone which the builders rejected." This "stone" is the One that "has become the chief cornerstone." He was speaking of Himself. Jesus is the chief cornerstone. The Apostles and prophets filled out the foundation (Eph 2:20; 1 Cor 3:5-15).

So not only is the confession that Jesus is the Christ, the Son of God, the rock upon which Jesus would build His church, but He Himself is the cornerstone.

VIII. THE ROCKS DID CRY OUT (MATTHEW 27:51, 54)

In his Gospel, Matthew includes the Triumphal Entry. However, unlike Luke, he does not specifically mention the fact that Jesus said at that time that if His disciples had not cried out, "the stones would immediately cry out" (Luke 19:40). But Matthew does cite John the Baptist who indicates that "God is able to raise up children to Abraham from these stones" (Matt 3:9).

When Jesus died, the stones did cry out in a figurative sense. As the rocks were split (Matt 27:51), they were confessing that Jesus is the Christ, the Son of God. The centurion heard the "voice" of the rocks and he confessed, "Truly this was the Son of God!" (Matt 27:54).

IX. CONCLUSION

There is a clear connection in Matthew's Gospel, indeed, in all of the Gospels, between the stone, rock, and tomb motifs. Jesus is regularly associated with these three themes. They emphasize and confess that Jesus is the Christ, the Son of God.

Faith in Jesus as the Christ results in eternal life. Our confession of Him as the Christ, the Son of God, is itself a rock upon which Jesus builds His church. Jesus Himself is the cornerstone for the Church. A life built on Jesus' teachings is like a house built on bedrock. It will not be moved by the calamities we all face in life, even when we face death itself.

THE SOVEREIGNTY OF GOD: CONTEMPORARY EVANGELICAL ATTESTATION VERSUS BIBLICAL ATTESTATION

JEREMY D. EDMONDSON

I. INTRODUCTION

God is sovereign, a truth clearly stated in Scripture: "Your faithfulness endures to all generations; you have established the earth, and it stands fast. By your appointment they stand this day, for all things are your servants" (Ps 119:90-91, ESV). But as with any statement, terms must be defined. What is meant by "sovereign" may not always be agreed upon, even though the word is commonly found in contemporary Evangelicalism. The purpose of this article is to prove by an examination of modern information, brief historical documentation, and an exegesis of pertinent Scripture passages that the Biblical explanation and the contemporary, Evangelical assertion of the use(s) of the word "sovereign" in describing God differ greatly. This divide leads to unbiblical conclusions in Christian thinking, portraying God as the author of sin and man as a passive puppet. Our view of the character of God must be formed according to divine revelation; this will produce right thinking about God and will guide us to understand the actions that properly represent His name. Thus, the very doctrine of theology proper is at stake.

II. CONTEMPORARY EVANGELICAL EVIDENCE

The modern-day definitions of the "sovereignty of God" have come from those who would largely be considered Reformed in their theological disposition. Steve Lawson quotes R.C. Sproul in stating that "sovereign" means "That God is in charge and that God is in control of all things."[1] "To determine the destiny and the route of all

---

[1] Steve Lawson, "Our Sovereign God," Filmed [2009]. YouTube Video, 48:22. Posted June 17, 2015. See https://www.youtube.com/watch?v=5D83eBjKebY,

that is under His purview, sovereignty is an attribute of deity without which God would not be God." He notes that "sovereignty" means that God is "above or superior to all others. Chief, greatest, supreme; supreme in power, rank and authority; holding the position of ruler and despot, independent of all others."[2]

Lawson's understanding is that God should be understood as the "Supreme Controller" of all things and that nothing occurs apart from His endorsement or cause. "Sometimes we need to be reminded by God himself that there are no limits to his rule," writes John Piper. "We need to hear from him that he is sovereign over the whole world, and everything that happens in it."[3] Piper also sees God as a "Supreme Controller" over "everything that happens."

In an article entitled "Prayer and the Sovereignty of God," John Hannah asks the question, "If God has absolutely decreed all that can and will come to pass to the smallest detail in the lives of every human being, does prayer change things?"[4] It is clear from the article's title and the nature of the question posed that Hannah understands the sovereignty of God to be synonymous with the notion that He has foreordained every single act that will ever happen, down to the finest detail. Again, we see the theme of "Supreme Controller."

A. W. Pink falls in step with this assertion:

> To say that God is sovereign is to declare that He is the Almighty and the owner of all power in Heaven and earth. No one can defeat His plans, prevent His purpose, or resist His will (Psalms 115:3). To say that God is sovereign is to proclaim that He is "The Governor among the nations" (Psalms 22:28), setting up kingdoms, overthrowing empires, and determining the pathway of dynasties as He decides what is best. To say that God is sovereign is to announce that He is the "Only Potentate, the King of kings, and Lord of lords" (1 Timothy 6:15). This is the real picture of the God of the Bible.[5]

2:18-2:23. Accessed Sept. 16, 2016.

[2] Ibid., 16:17-17:00.

[3] John Piper, "Plunge Your Mind into the Ocean of God's Sovereignty," Desiring God, Dec. 1, 2015. https://www.desiringgod.org/articles/plunge-your-mind-into-the-ocean-of-god-s-sovereignty. Accessed Sept. 15, 2016.

[4] John D. Hannah, "Prayer and the Sovereignty of God," *Bibliotheca Sacra* 136/4 (1979): 351.

[5] Arthur W. Pink, *The Sovereignty of God* (Alachua, FL: Bridge-Logos, 2008), 8.

Pink's definition of God's sovereignty also affirms His rule as having an undeterred purpose and certain plan for the existence of the universe. However, he also calls for God's sovereignty to include the idea that He is the "owner of all power in Heaven and earth," and that He determines "the pathway of dynasties." Pink's view is not only that God is a Supreme Ruler, but also a "Supreme Controller" of every minute detail of existence.

This notion of "Supreme Controller" is overflowing in Christian books, periodicals, and pulpits, without any allowance of variation regarding how God's sovereignty is exercised. The modern-day definition of the "sovereignty of God" has gone past the idea of "Ruler" or "King" and into the realm of "Divine Puppeteer." Is this how we should think about the Creator of the universe? Does "sovereignty" equal a meticulous control over every decision and movement in creation? "'Absolute sovereignty' is a redundancy, because sovereignty rightly understood is always absolute," writes Robert Thomas. "It is the same as using 'very unique' to describe a phenomenon, because if something is unique, only one degree of uniqueness exists."[6] Is such a conclusion derived from Biblical exegesis, or could it have been influenced by the writings of teachers in the past?

III. HISTORICAL THEOLOGICAL CONSIDERATIONS

The Bible is not a systematic theology book, although it contains all of the elements that one would need in order to form one's theology systematically. Instead, it is a progressive revelation beginning with God as the Creator. Understandably, many of the doctrines that we take for granted today were the labors of godly men and women who sought to understand the Lord to a greater degree by relentlessly poring over the Scriptures so as to gather all of the information contained in them for the purpose of categorization. Two of the greatest contributors to church history are Augustine and John Calvin, especially in regards to the formulation of the doctrine of God's sovereignty. Between their views, an interesting progression takes place. Rigby explains:

---

[6] Robert Thomas, "The Hermeneutics of 'Open Theism,'" *The Master's Seminary Journal*, 12/2 (2001): 195.

In the fourth century, Augustine argued that human beings have free will, explaining that God does not cause us to act in a particular way but, rather, foreknows what decisions we will make. In the sixteenth century, Calvin taught that everything that happens is willed by God, but human beings are nonetheless culpable for evil because they are not intending, when they sin, to serve God's will (*Institutes*, 1.17.5). Concerned to uphold both the divine sovereignty and human agency, the Westminster Confession (1647) explains that God is the first cause who ordains everything that comes to pass, including the fact that we, as secondary causes, exercise discreet volition and creative powers (6.014).[7]

John Calvin's view of God's sovereignty led him to logically conclude that God's meticulous foreordination and supreme control over all existence consequently make Him the responsible party for the world's ills:

> From this it is easy to conclude how foolish and frail *is the support of divine justice afforded by the* suggestion that evils come to be not by [God's] will, but merely by his permission. Of course, so far as they are evils, which men perpetrate with their evil mind, as I shall show in greater detail shortly, I admit that they are not pleasing to God. But it is a quite frivolous refuge to say that God permits them, when Scripture shows Him not only willing but the author of them.[8]

Such a view is logically conclusive from the views and quotations that have been previously seen. However, such a claim, if it is true, raises questions regarding the purity of God's character and His disposition toward the world.

Rigby's short summation coupled with Calvin's conclusion marks the cliff over which the boundaries of God's sovereignty were firmly pushed, falling to a tragic conclusion: The God of the universe, Creator of all things, controls the world in such a way that He wills the very sin that has separated Him from man.

Lest we conclude that this view was the only acceptable conclusion for Christian orthodoxy, other views on the doctrine of God's sovereignty are also found in history. An example is *The Waterland*

[7]Cynthia L. Rigby, "Free to be Human: Limits, Possibilities, and the Sovereignty of God," *Theology Today* 53/1 (Apr 1996): 48.

[8]John Calvin, *Concerning the Eternal Predestination of God* (Kindle Edition, N.P: n.d.), 176.

Confession (1580), a confession that was originally drawn up by the Mennonites in the Netherlands and was later republished at the request of John Smyth in 1610. Regarding God's sovereignty, it reads:

> God foresaw and foreknew all things which have come to pass, are coming to pass, and shall come to pass both good and evil, but since he is only perfect good and the fountain of life, we believe and confess that he is the sole Author, Origin, and Operator of those things which are good, holy, sincere, pure and which agree with his nature; but not at all of sins and damnable evils. For God enjoins that which is good; he desires that we obey him in that which is good; he consults for and admonishes to it, and makes great promises to those who obey. On the contrary he forbids evil, exhorts against evil, threatens evil doers, and denounces against them eternal punishment. And by this means shows himself to be an enemy of sinners and that all iniquity is contrary to his holy nature. And therefore, not God who is good, but man who is evil, by voluntarily choosing sin to which the spirit of wickedness leads him, which is dominant in him, is the author, origin and operator of sins and all wickedness, and for this reason is worthy of punishment.[9]

This confession stood as a model for the General Baptists of later generations in England. While some may be swayed to disregard this confession due to its Arminian leanings, one must admit that the quoted portion keeps the sound integrity and holy character of God intact and free from any accusations of sin. Thus, His holy character and righteous standards are preserved without Scriptural or logical conflict.

IV. THEOLOGICAL EXAMINATIONS

As we have seen in Rigby's comments, many have sought to rationalize the concept that God is ultimately responsible for sin by making a distinction between "primary" and "secondary causes." Such language is found to be duplicitous. R.C. Sproul explains this "relationship":

> "Second causes" are *secondary*, and as such are dependent on a *primary* cause for their potency. God, and God alone, is the sole

---

[9]William L. Lumpkin, *Baptist Confessions of Faith* (Valley Forge, PA: Judson Press, 1969), 46.

primary cause in the universe… He is the *ground* of all causal power. Scripture declares that in God "we live and move and have our being" (Acts 17:28). God is the ground of all being, all life, and all motion. Apart from his power to create and sustain life, no life is possible. Apart from his power of being, nothing else would be or could be. Apart from his power of motion (primary causality), nothing can move, change, act, or bring about effects… God not only reigns, but also rules, and he rules sovereignly. Secondary causes are not, however, imaginary or impotent. They exert real causal power. We make real choices. Yet a secondary cause is always dependent on the primary cause, God himself, for its efficacy. God brings to pass his sovereign will through or by means of secondary causes. "By means of" is another way of saying that God ordains not only the *ends,* but also the *means* to these ends (emphasis original).[10]

This concept can also be seen in the *Philadelphia Baptist Confession of Faith.*

Although in relation to the foreknowledge and decree of God, the first cause, all things come to pass immutably and infallibly; so that there is not anything befalls any by chance or without His providence; yet by the same providence He ordereth them to fall out according to the nature of second causes, either necessarily, freely, or contingently."[11]

This confession's use of the word "ordereth" reveals that God is just as much behind the secondary causes of sin as He is behind the primary. According to Sproul's explanation, secondary causes cannot operate apart from their primary cause. When a scapegoat like "secondary causes" is put forth, an excuse is given for mankind being manipulated by God to be the dispenser of sin and yet is found to be unapologetically culpable for that which mankind could not do otherwise. This conclusion paints a malicious picture of a deceitful God. One cannot help but conclude that God's "ordination" of the means and the end (according to Sproul) makes Him directly responsible for every instance of rape, murder, robbery, automobile accident, extramarital affair, arson, and hunger that has ever occurred in history.

---

[10] R.C. Sproul, *What is Reformed Theology? Understanding the Basics* (Grand Rapids, MI: Baker Books, 1997), 173-74.

[11] *Philadelphia Baptist Confession of Faith* (Asheville, NC: Revival Literature, 2007), 26.

A. Scriptural Distortions

Does this view spring from a correct handling of the Scriptures? In quoting Isa 46:9 (in the video, he says Isa 6:9, but that is an obvious mistake), Steve Lawson declares that "all is foreordained by God."[12] But is this what Isa 46:9 says? When the context is considered, we see that there is no one and nothing that is like God (v 9), that He "declares" the end from the beginning and can pronounce prophecy which will be accomplished according to His purposes (v 10). If God has spoken about something, He will surely bring it to fruition (v 11). God moves history as He sees fit and has complete foreknowledge of all events. Lawson's understanding of "declares" in 46:10 is "foreordains." The word *maggid* in Hebrew means "declare, make known, expound, especially of something before not understood, concealed or mysterious,"[13] and never speaks to the idea of foreordination. Thus, Lawson's conclusion is unfounded.

Another instance can be seen in the writings of James White, a Reformed apologist and theologian. In providing a Biblical explanation of God's sovereignty, he writes:

> God is king over all the earth. As the Creator, it is His to do with as *He* chooses. This concept is brought out with striking clarity in the analogy of the Potter and the clay. A number of times in Scripture God likens Himself to a Potter and we as clay or as pots, formed and fashioned as He wishes. This sovereign power is seen in God's dealings with Israel. He sent Jeremiah the prophet to the potter's house and recorded this incident in Jeremiah 18:4-6:
>
>> But the vessel that he was making of clay was spoiled in the hand of the potter; so he remade it into another vessel, as it pleased the potter to make. Then the word of the Lord came to me saying, "Can I not, O house of Israel, deal with you as this potter *does?*" declares the Lord. "Behold, like the clay in the potter's hand, so are you in My hand, O house of Israel.
>
> God could fashion and remake Israel as He pleased. He did not have to ask permission, seek advice, or in any way consult anyone

---

[12]Lawson, "Our Sovereign God," 25:58-26:04.

[13]Francis Brown, Samuel Rolles Driver, and Charles Augustus Briggs, *Enhanced Brown-Driver-Briggs Hebrew and English Lexicon* (Oxford, ENG: Clarendon Press, 1977), 616. Hereafter known as BDB.

or anything outside of Himself. The entire nation was as clay in the potter's hand. Clay has no inherent "rights," no basis upon which to complain about the potter's decisions, no say in what the potter does (emphasis original).[14]

What is not readily apparent in White's argument is that he has stopped short of representing God fully as the text portrays Him. No one would argue with the fact that God does not need the counsel of another, nor would any Bible student conclude that God cannot do as He chooses. But in reading this passage further, one can clearly see in Jer 18:7-11 that God will withhold a kingdom or nation's destruction if the people will repent (vv 7-8), just as He will reconsider the good that He had planned for a kingdom or nation if it does evil (vv 9-10). The Lord then calls upon Jeremiah to cry out to Judah for repentance because of the calamity that He is personally fashioning against them for their disobedience (v 11).

Thus, God is sovereign in that He rules and is able to bring about destruction and blessing upon a kingdom or nation. Yet the text clearly shows that such an end is determined by the inhabitants' response to God's Word in acknowledging God's sovereignty and in repenting in light of it.

B. Contemporary Views of God and His Relationship to Sin

What is most troubling in this distorted understanding of the "sovereignty of God" is that theologians and scholars have no issue with attributing the ultimate responsibility of sin and its effects in the world to God. For instance, Doran writes:

> The Scriptures also teach that even the sinful acts of the devil and men are under His control so that He accomplishes His purposes. The biblical record regarding Satan's attacks against Job proves this. Satan had to have permission from God: "Then the Lord said to Satan, 'Behold, all that he has is in your power, only do not put forth your hand on him.' So Satan departed from the presence of the Lord" (Job 1:12); "So the Lord said to Satan, 'Behold, he is in your power, only spare his life'" (Job 2:6). This is confirmed by Job's

---

[14] James R. White, *The Potter's Freedom: A Defense of the Reformation and a Rebuttal to Norman Geisler's* Chosen But Free (N.P.: Calvary Press Publishing, 2009), 43-44.

response recorded in Job 1:20–21: "Then Job arose and tore his robe and shaved his head, and he fell to the ground and worshiped. He said, 'Naked I came from my mother's womb, and naked I shall return there. The Lord gave and the Lord has taken away. Blessed be the name of the Lord.'"[15]

God in no way controlled the specific acts that Satan committed against Job; He only set the boundaries. God's allowance of sin is certainly not the same as God's causing sin. While God can constrain sin, or choose not to, and while He can take a sinful situation and bring about a conclusion that gives Him glory (Gen 50:20), such choices do not make God the cause, originator, or author of sin.

However, Doran's conclusion is also shared by John Piper. Quoting him from a seminar held in 2012, author Anugrah Kumar writes, "Herod's mockery, Pilate's expediency, the Gentiles driving the nails, and the people of Israel shouting, 'Crucify Him, crucify Him,' is all sin, Piper said, adding it was all 'predestined, designed by God, scripted in the Old Testament, including Judas [Iscariot].'"[16] While the Scriptures are clear that the crucifixion of Christ was an event ordained in order to save the world, Acts 4:27-28 says nothing of God's being responsible for the actions of Herod, Pilate, the Gentiles, or the Jews. God was not responsible for their sin, and He did not force their hand. Claiming otherwise has serious ramifications on the very definition of what is considered "good" in any moral sense. If Piper's conclusions were true, how could anyone ever truly trust God?

C. Inconsistent Logic in Light of the Scriptures

When God declares that something is "good" (Gen 1:4, 10, 12, 18, 21, 25, 31), He is making a moral declaration that sets the standard for what is "good." For instance, Paul argues that the Law is considered "good" (Rom 7:16; 1 Tim 1:8) in that it is the written perfection of God which He uses to show us our sin (Rom 3:20). However, if God causes, promotes, or advocates sin (which is something the Word of God has clearly portrayed as the opposite of "good"—see, e.g., Matt

---

[15]David M. Doran, "God's Sovereignty and the Spread of the Gospel," *Detroit Baptist Seminary Journal* 9/9 (2004): 187.

[16]Anugrah Kumar, "John Piper on Man's Sin and God's Sovereignty," *Christian Post*. See http://www.christianpost.com/news/john-piper-on-mans-sin-and-gods-sovereignty-80617/. Accessed Sept. 21, 2016.

1:21; 18:15; John 5:14; Rom 5:12; 6:23)—we would be forced to include "sin" in the definition of what is understood as "good," because God condones it for His glory. Therefore, a statement such as, "Be holy, for I am holy" (Lev 11:44; 1 Pet 1:16) would necessarily include our employment of sin for this end, if we are to be like God.

In addition, if God condones sin for His glory, such statements as, "What is this that you have done?" (Gen 3:13) and "Sin is crouching at the door. Its desire is for you, but you must rule over it" (Gen 4:7) are seen to be contradictory moral statements. Such statements would need to be changed to, "You have done exactly as My sovereignty has predestined you to do," and "Sin is crouching at the door because I put it there. Let it do its evil work for My glory." As anyone can determine, such conclusions are both ludicrous and blasphemous.

Setting such horrendous notions aside, L. Russ Bush offers a more balanced and Biblical conclusion:

> Apparently, God has sovereignly chosen to allow (and thus to create) a reality within which some real freedom exists within limits, but the future is not therefore open ended. The reason one knows that God has not determined everything is that God's will is not always done. God is not willing that any should perish (2 Pet. 3:9), but some do (2 Thess. 2:10). God is not a sinner and does not cause sin (1 John 3:3–5), but sin occurs nonetheless. Adam was given the choice to eat or not to eat, an existential and morally significant choice. Adam, not God, was responsible for the choice that he made... His choice was real, but there was not an unlimited range of possible futures. So it is with all choices and futures.[17]

D. Resisting God's Will?

Before we conclude that the assertion "God's will is not always done" is implausible, we must consider that this was Stephen's conclusion just before his execution at the hands of the Sanhedrin. What ignited the rage that led to his martyrdom was the statement,

> You stiff-necked people, uncircumcised in heart and ears, you always resist the Holy Spirit. As your fathers did, so do you. Which of the prophets did your fathers not persecute? And they killed those who announced beforehand the coming of the Righteous One, whom

---

[17]L. Russ Bush, "Open Theism: Good Try, But No Dice," *Faith and Mission* 21/2 (2003), 26.

you have now betrayed and murdered, you who received the law as delivered by angels and did not keep it (Acts 7:51-53).

Not only is there the blatant declaration that the Jews were always resisting the Holy Spirit (attributing the reason for this to their stiff necks, uncircumcised hearts, and uncircumcised ears [7:51]), but a second instance is cited in that they did not keep the Law once they had received it (7:53).

This idea is also found in a statement spoken through the tears of the Messiah. Jesus laments over Jerusalem's past aggression and rebellion against the prophets of God, but He also laments their present rejection of Him. He states, "O Jerusalem, Jerusalem, the city that kills the prophets and stones those who are sent to it! How often would I have gathered your children together as a hen gathers her brood under her wings, and you were not willing" (Matt 23:37). If no one resists God's will because of "God's sovereignty," why would Jesus (being God) purposefully orchestrate such a scenario that would bring Him great sorrow in decreeing the rejection of the Jewish people? Such an action is clearly against the declarations of His loyal love for the Jewish people. Scripture is clear that Jesus is weeping because Israel is responsible for their national rejection of their promised Messiah and would reap the consequences of those actions. While many other instances could be cited, these are sufficient.

V. VARIATIONS IN TRANSLATION

How have the historical views of the sovereignty of God and the theology that has proceeded from them affected the translation of God's Word? The answer is found in an examination of popular translations and by noting the variations with each one.

A. The Use of "Sovereign" in Formal Equivalence Translations

In the King James Version (KJV), the words "sovereign" and "sovereignty" are absent. The New King James Version (NKJV) yields no occurrences of "sovereign" and only one instance of "sovereignty." It is found in 1 Sam 14:47 and is used to replace the word "kingdom" as used in the KJV, which speaks of King Saul establishing his kingdom over Israel.

The New American Standard Bible (NASB) finds one occurrence of "sovereign" (1 Tim 6:15) and seven uses of "sovereignty," five of which are found in Daniel (4:31, 36; 5:18; 7:27; 11:4). The English Standard Version (ESV) shows only three occurrences of "sovereign" (Acts 4:24; 1 Tim 6:15; Rev 6:10) and no occurrences of "sovereignty." Regarding older, literal translations, Young's (1862) shows no instances of "sovereign" or "sovereignty," while Darby's (1890) has one use of "sovereign" (Rev 6:10) and two uses of "sovereignty" (1 Kings 21:7; Dan 2:44).[18]

B. The Use of "Sovereign" in Dynamic Equivalence Translations

By contrast, in the New International Version (NIV), the word "sovereign" turns up 303 times, of which only five are found in the NT. The word "sovereignty" yields two instances, both occurring in Daniel (5:18; 7:27), and neither refers to God. The New Living Translation (NLT) has 294 occurrences of "sovereign," with three appearing in the NT, while the word "sovereignty" occurs four times, all in the book of Daniel (2:37; 5:18; 7:14, 27), with Daniel 7:14 speaking of sovereignty granted to the Lord Jesus. The New English Translation (NET) tallies 368 uses of the word "sovereign," with four instances occurring in the NT, and seven uses of "sovereignty," with only one occurrence in the NT (Rev 17:18).

C. Conclusion of Translation Findings

The dynamic equivalence translations have promoted an escalation of the use of "sovereign" and "sovereignty" in their versions, something which the formal equivalence translations do not have. This difference is not a subtle departure. The dynamic equivalence translators have gone to great lengths in using "sovereign" and "sovereignty"

---

[18]The Holman Christian Standard Bible (HCSB) which is considered by many to be a moderate dynamic equivalence (and has been promoted as an "optimal equivalence") shows only one occurrence of "sovereign" (1 Tim 6:15) and five instances of "sovereignty," all occurring in the OT. See Lifeway Staff, "The Holman Christian Standard Bible Translation Philosophy," Lifeway. http://www.lifeway.com/Article/bible-hcsb-the-Holman-Christian-Standard-Bible-translation-philosophy. Accessed Dec. 15, 2015.

to the point that the words are extraneous.[19] Clearly there has been a great change since the days of the Reformation, for the KJV would have been considered the most well known formal equivalence relative to that time, and yet these words cannot be found within its pages.

VI. BIBLICAL EVIDENCE AND MEANING

It would be helpful to consider what Hebrew and Greek words were translated as "sovereign" and "sovereignty" in the Old and New Testaments. The single occurrence of "sovereignty" in the NKJV is 1 Sam 14:47; it speaks of King Saul, and the original Hebrew uses the word *melukāh,* which means "kingship, royalty."[20] In discussing this word, Brown-Driver-Briggs (BDB) gives no consideration to the idea of "supreme controller," nor to any thought of a meticulous foreordination of everything that will ever occur. The NASB lists 1 Tim 6:15 as the only use of the word "sovereign" which translates the Greek *dynastēs,* "one who is in a high or exalted position."[21]

In the ESV, the translators of Acts 4:24 and Rev 6:10 use the words "Sovereign Lord" to render the Greek *despotēs*—"one who has legal control and authority over persons, such as subjects or slaves" or "one who controls a thing."[22] The Reformed theologian might claim that these verses, and the Greek word, support their view of the word

---

[19]The NIV (1978), NLT (1996), and NET (2005), all of which are dynamic equivalence translations, display the greatest occurrences of the words in question, which leads one to believe that a loose method of translation lends itself to a distortion of the Scriptures, at least in a manner that the formal equivalence translation committees did not consider as viable words to use in capturing the essence of the original languages. For instance, the ESV has undergone two revisions since its initial release in 2001 (2007, 2011), both of which did not cause the translators to change any of the revised portions to reflect the use of "sovereign" or "sovereignty" because there was no lack of clarity in what was meant in the original languages. It can be concluded that the words "sovereign" and "sovereignty" in Scripture translations should be used sparingly in reflecting the original languages, as seen in the more accurate translations in the formal equivalence camp.

[20]BDB, 574.

[21]William Arndt, Frederick W. Danker, and Walter Bauer, *A Greek-English Lexicon of the New Testament and Other Early Christian Literature* (Chicago: University of Chicago Press, 2000), 264. Hereafter known as BDAG.

[22]Ibid., 220.

"sovereign." But the use of this word in Scripture sometimes refers to a "master" and his relationship to his servants (1 Tim 6:1-2; Titus 2:9; 1 Pet 2:18). None of these instances refer to God or Jesus Christ. The word can also simply mean "master" of a house (2 Tim 2:21), "Lord" as it refers to God (Luke 2:29), or "Master" as it refers to Jesus (2 Pet 2:1; Jude 4). None of these uses referring to Jesus or God give any indication of complete rule or meticulous foreordination. The translation of *despotēs* as "Sovereign Lord" is simply the translator's choice.

The Bible student should also question why the use of *despotēs* in Acts 4:24 and Rev 6:10 has been translated as "Sovereign Lord" when *kurios* (usually translated "Lord") is not found in either text. Thus, "Master" is a fine translation, but in no way does BDAG (or the context of each of the passages cited) lead the reader to understand the word *despotēs* to mean "complete, foreordained control."

The uses of "sovereignty" in the NASB are found in the book of Daniel. In 4:31, 36, and 5:18, variations of the word are translated as "kingship" and "kingdom." Each reference involves King Nebuchadnezzar. Daniel 7:27 reads:

> And the *kingdom* and the dominion
> and the greatness of the *kingdoms* under the whole heaven
> shall be given to the people of the saints of the Most High;
> his *kingdom* shall be an everlasting *kingdom*,
> and all dominions shall serve and obey him (NASB, emphasis added).

This passage speaks of a future time when the kingdoms (first two instances) under heaven will be given to the saints of God, and the kingdom of the Lord will stand forever with all other powers and authorities serving Him. Finally, Dan 11:4 uses the word "kingdom" twice; both instances refer to the future kingdom of Alexander the Great.

These occurrences are derived from the Hebrew root word *melek,* which means "royalty, reign, kingdom,"[23] and are political in nature. However, none of these uses speak to unswerving, meticulous foreordination or to a "supreme controller." Even in Dan 7:27, God's

---

[23]BDB, 1100. See also R. Laird Harris, Gleason L. Archer Jr., and Bruce K. Waltke, eds., *Theological Wordbook of the Old Testament* (Chicago: Moody Press, 1999), 1041.

"everlasting kingdom" is shown to be that which all "dominions" will "serve and obey." This says nothing of "supreme control." Gordon Olson considers this word's use in the OT:

> There is not a hint in any of these passages of any exhaustive direct control by which Yahweh decreed every event to take place in the universe. Indeed, the imagery of king and kingdom could not possibly communicate such an idea to ancient middle-eastern peoples unless it were spelled out explicitly. These terms were not only used for the rulers of great empires, but also for the heads of small cities and thus do not support such an idea. Not even the greatest kings exercised direct control of all events in their domain. Their decrees were carried out indirectly by government officials. Therefore, there is no way that direct control of all events by a sovereign could be indicated by the cultural usage of the words "king" or "kingdoms."[24]

VII. CONCLUSION

The purpose of this study is to prove by an examination of modern information, brief historical documentation, and an exegesis of pertinent Scripture passages that the Biblical explanation and the contemporary, Evangelical assertion of the word "sovereign" in describing God differ greatly. The provided documentation is sufficient to show that there is a cause for alarm. The Reformed position ultimately attributes sin's origin, presence, and effects to God by misrepresenting Scripture, and thus misrepresenting God.[25] Such views are not coherent, and the ramifications will impact the lives and ministry of those individuals who hold them. Earl Radmacher's comments strike at the heart of the matter:

> When one considers that basic to right action is right thinking and that basic to right thinking is right thinking about what God is

---

[24]C. Gordon Olson, *Beyond Calvinism and Arminianism: An Inductive Mediate Theology of Salvation* (Lynchburg, VA: Global Gospel Publishers, 2012), 31.

[25]Editor's note: For most readers of the *JOTGES* it will be recognized that this has a dramatic impact on the gospel of eternal life. If the Reformed/Calvinist view of soteriology is correct, then God has ordained who will believe and who will not. That is, God has chosen who will receive eternal life and who will not. As a result, none of us can have assurance of eternal life since none of us can ever know if God has pre-determined that we would be His children.

like, it begins to become transparently clear that our generation, or any other, will never begin to solve its problems until it corrects its ideas about God.[26]

In examining the pertinent Bible passages, we have observed that the words "sovereign" and "sovereignty" refer to the idea of a "king" and/or a "kingdom," and at no time do the Scriptures allow for an understanding that communicates the idea of "Supreme Controller" or the "meticulous foreordination of all events." An unbalanced understanding of God's sovereignty has certainly been found to be zealous but cannot be considered Biblical.

---

[26]Earl D. Radmacher, Book Review. "Our Sovereign God: Addresses Presented to the Philadelphia Conference on Reformed Theology." *Journal of the Evangelical Theological Society* 21/3 (Sept 1978): 265. http://web.b.ebscohost.com.ezproxy. liberty.edu:2048/ehost/pdfviewer/pdfviewer?vid=4&sid=bcba3d41-132e-4ec9-8c27-f0fbe61b3ed7%40sessionmgr114&hid=123. Accessed Nov. 5, 2015.

FREE AT LAST![1] FREEDOM IN JESUS' FOOTSTEPS (JOHN 8:30-32)

JOHN H. NIEMELÄ

President
Message of Life Ministries

I. INTRODUCTION

As Jesus taught, some retorted in John 8:33 with their own question:

They answered Him, "We are Abraham's descendants, and have never been in bondage to anyone. How *can* You say, 'You will be made free?'"[2] (NKJV)

Knowing who asked this question is vital. Did the new believers of vv 30-32 turn against Jesus? The answer to this matter affects both the meaning of John 8:30-32 and the believer's security.

II. JESUS TEACHING IN THE TEMPLE

Before identifying the speakers in John 8:33, one must consider its context. Where was Jesus? What was He doing? Was the crowd that listened to Him unified or composed of opposing groups?

While Jesus was *teaching* in the temple courts (see John 8:20), He spoke the words of 8:14-18 to counter a false testimony charge leveled against Him in v 13. This is the first of a series of questions by

---

[1] The author read an earlier version of this paper at the GES conference on April 25, 2013. The following, each written by John H. Niemelä, also derive from it: "Who Spoke? John 8:30-33," *Grace in Focus* (July-Aug, 2013): 15; "Who Can Abide?" *Grace in Focus* (Sept–Oct 2013): 12, 15; "Who Objected? John 8:30-33," *Grace in Focus* (Nov–Dec 2013): 15. Thanks to Kenneth Yates, Richard Christianson, Lon Gregg, and Frank Tyler for giving feedback on this article.

[2] Unless otherwise noted, all Scripture renderings are the author's.

hecklers interrupting Jesus as He taught receptive crowds at the same time. John 8:33 is the fifth of ten disruptions (8:13, 19a, 22, 25a, 33, 39a, 41b, 48, 52-53, and 57).

The verb *teach* (v 20) always takes two (explicit or implicit) objects. One teaches (1) *someone* and (2) *something.* For example, "I teach (1) seminarians (2) Greek." Jesus encountered heckling while He was teaching receptive crowds. But at the same time, He taught content.

Perhaps a modern example will clarify the circumstances. Marriage seminars are teaching events for responsive hearers, but interrupting hecklers who reject Biblical definitions of marriage sometimes infiltrate. Attendees might say, "The speaker said these things (refuting hecklers), as he was teaching us." This mentions a teacher, the content of his teaching, hecklers, and us (fellow attentive learners).

John 8:12-59 occurs after the account of the woman caught in the act of adultery. Determining who remained with Jesus in the treasury after the woman's accusers left is important. Verse 9b hints that the original crowd stayed: "Only Jesus and the woman (being *in the midst of the crowd*) was left" (emphasis mine). Notably, even those who omit the account of the woman caught in adultery (7:53–8:11) recognize two types of people present throughout chap. 8. One group consists of teachable people who were interested in what Jesus was teaching them. The other group consists of those opposed to Him (including hecklers).

The receptive crowds are the "elephant in the room" that most expositors ignore. They imagine a 100% hostile crowd and scoff at *any* (much less *many*) actually believing in Him. Yet John 8:30 says, "many believed in Him." By twisting this into *so-called believers,* commentaries equate new believers with hecklers in 8:33. How do expositors miss this elephant? John 8:20 implies the presence of a teachable group of people in the temple that morning.

Consider what Jesus taught in 8:12 to the many receptive listeners:

> Jesus *again* spoke *to them*,[3] "I am the Light of the world. He who follows Me never will walk in darkness, but will have the light of life" (emphasis mine).

---

[3] Wilbur N. Pickering, "What Difference Does it Make? The Greek Text We Accept Makes a Big Difference," *JOTGES* 25 (Spring 2012): 54ff, shows that omitting 7:53–8:11 leaves no reasonable antecedent for *them* when, in 8:12, Jesus spoke to *them* a second time ("He said to *them* again…").

It is true that Pharisees did heckle Him in v 13 for what He said in v 12. Even so, glimpses of His teaching appear in 8:12 and 31f. The latter tells of Jesus addressing believers:

> Then Jesus told *Judeans*[4] *who believed* in Him, "If you abide in My word, truly you are My disciples. And you shall know the truth and the truth shall free you" (8:31-32, emphasis mine).

The contrast between the Pharisees and the crowd in general is striking. The former avoided Him by leaving (8:9a) or opposed Him by repeatedly arguing (8:13, 19a, 22, 25a, 33, 39a, 41b, 48, 52-53, 57) and by trying to stone Him (8:59).

Though John focuses on exchanges between Jesus and the hecklers, this is *not* a debate context. John 8:20 calls it a teaching setting, which was interrupted by hecklers. Remembering the elephant in the room is crucial. John characterizes this as a day of teaching.

Sadly, most of Christendom is in the dark over John 8:12, 30-32. Expositors foist these verses onto unbelievers, claiming that abiding (persevering) is a requisite to gaining (or keeping) eternal life. Thus, they deny faith alone in Jesus Christ alone for eternal life.

Instead, the challenge for the hearers to abide (8:31-32) addresses Christians—John specifically says that those Jesus was speaking to had believed in Him (v 30). All believers have everlasting life, but His truth frees those believers who abide in His word.

III. THREE VIEWS OF JOHN 8:30-33

Jesus' words in 8:12-29 prompted opposite responses. Some responded in faith (v 30). However, others rejected what Jesus said and were hecklers (v 33).

Lively debate today exists over whether there is a break between 8:32 and 8:33; the outcome of this debate determines who is speaking in 8:33. A related issue has also resulted in disagreement—it is whether the "believers" in 8:30-32 have everlasting life. There are basically three views of this passage.

---

[4] Josiah S. Bisbee, "The Gospel according to John: To What Realm Do *Ioudaioi* Belong?" (Th.M. Thesis: Rocky Mountain Seminary, 2011), argues convincingly that *Ioudaios* in John means "Judean," not "Jew."

One view is that there is no break between 8:32 and 8:33. The speakers of 8:33 would be those who believed, but they have a "faith that fails" and would thus be unsaved. One could call this the unity/unsaved view.[5]

A second view is that there is a break between 8:32 and 8:33. The speakers of 8:33 are different from the believers of 8:30-32. However, the believers have a "faith that may fail" and would thus be unsaved. This is the break/unsaved view.

The third view is that there is a break between 8:32 and 8:33. The speakers of 8:33 are different from the believers mentioned in the previous verses. However, the believers are saved even if their faith fails. This can be called the break/saved view.

Many expositors know of only two of the three views. Some are unaware that view three exists. Others do not know of view two. Thus, it would surprise many that Augustine held view two.[6]

Calvin wrestled with whether or not a break exists between 8:32 and 8:33.[7]

> It is uncertain whether the Evangelist is here [John 8:33] introducing the same people speaking or others. I think they replied to Christ confusedly, as usually happens in a mixed crowd, and that they were despisers rather than believers.[8]

Calvin imagined that believers must persevere in the faith in order to be true believers:

---

[5] This is the default position of commentaries. Finding advocates of this view is easy. This article cites Calvin and Hendriksen (because their comments are noteworthy), but the view is widely held.

[6] Augustine, *In Iohannis Evangelium Tractatus*, 41.2, accepted a break between 8:32 and 8:33. However, he linked 8:31b: "If you abide in My word, truly you are My disciples" to Matt 10:22b, "He who endures to the end, this one shall be saved;" ibid., 41:1. He took *saved* there as a reference to being saved from hell. This is view two. Calvin also considered view two (8:32/33 break; unsaved) but favored view one (no break in 8:32-33; unsaved). See John Calvin, *The Gospel According to St. John: 1–10*, Calvin's Commentaries, trans. T. H. L. Parker, ed. D. W. and T. F. Torrance (Grand Rapids, MI: Eerdmans, 1961), 220*ff.*

[7] Calvin, *John: 1–10*, 220, dismisses the validity of faith in 8:30: "...the Evangelist imprecisely calls faith what was only a sort of preparation for faith... And the next warning [v 33] also refers to this." Thus, he rejected the 8:32/33 break and regarded the believers of v 30 as unbelievers.

[8] Ibid., 222.

Here [8:31] Christ first warns them that it is not enough for anyone to begin well if he does not correspondingly progress to the end... He distinguishes His followers from hypocrites by the mark that those who falsely proclaimed they believed, give way from the very start... whereas believers persevere to the winning-post.[9]

Calvin only pondered view one (32-33 unity, unsaved) versus view two (32-33 break, unsaved). He accused Scripture of lying by calling unbelievers believers: "the Evangelist imprecisely calls [this in 8:30] faith..."[10]

Persuading people of a break between 8:32/33 is only part of the battle. Those with a perseverance model will concoct ways to insert perseverance into this passage, imitating Augustine's view (8:32/33 break, unsaved).

IV. DOES A BREAK OCCUR BETWEEN JOHN 8:32 AND 33?

Hendriksen denies any break, claiming that only one group exists:

The entire section [8:30-38] is an uninterrupted story: those who in verse 30 are described as having believed in him are the same as those who oppose him vehemently in the verses which follow. There is no transition from one group to another. The people who are described in verses 30 and 31 do not have *genuine* faith...neither of these verses [33 or 37] indicates a transition *from one group to another group.* Verse 33 begins with the words, "*They* answered him." Naturally, the "they" refers to the people addressed in verse [31].[11] [emphasis in original]

Hendriksen challenges anyone to disprove his denial that any break between 8:32 and 8:33 exists. However, those who hold to view three have four reasons for maintaining that such a break does exist and that John transitions back to the opposing hecklers in 8:33.

---

[9] Ibid., 220*ff.*

[10] Ibid., 220.

[11] William Hendriksen, *Exposition of the Gospel According to John*, NTC (Grand Rapids, MI: Baker, 1954), 2:50*ff.* Most of the commentary literature denies a break between 8:32 and 33.

The first reason is that God's word never calls unbelievers believers.[12] The second is that clearer antecedents can supercede nearer antecedents in John.[13] The third is that those in 8:30ff do not merely *claim* to have faith. The Bible calls them believers.[14] Finally, belief in vv 30-32 followed by instantaneous rejection in v 33 defies all logic and reason.[15]

Calvinists champion Hendriksen's thesis and simply dismiss the rebuttals. Debbie Hunn, an advocate of view three, concedes that John's words *seem* to allow options:

> John 8:30-59…begins with the many who believed in Jesus in 8:30, ends with people trying to stone him in 8:59, and *gives no clear indication of when or even whether the subject changes between these two verses.*[16]

These apparent options arise because of certain facts within the verses. Verse 30 says that many believed in Jesus. The Lord addresses the "Judeans who believed in Him," in v 31. Verse 33 does not define *they* ("they replied").[17]

Most view-three advocates reluctantly admit that the above facts *allow, but do not require* that there is a break between 8:32 and 8:33. By contrast, this article asserts boldly that John's wording *demands*

---

[12] Zane C. Hodges, *The Gospel Under Siege: Faith and Works in Tension*, 2nd ed. (Dallas, TX: Redención Viva, 1992), 41-44.

[13] Richard W. Christianson, "The Soteriological Significance of *Pisteuō* in the Gospel of John," (Th.M. thesis: Grace Theological Seminary, 1987), 182ff; Debbie Hunn, "Who are 'They' in John 8:33," *Catholic Biblical Quarterly* 66, no. 4, (June 2004), 396ff; Joseph C. Dillow, *Final Destiny* (Monument, CO: Paniym, 2012), 358, n. 1230 (Several editions of that book exist. The pagination and note numbers differ slightly between editions. Consult his Scripture index for the page number in your copy). The clearer antecedent argument perceives that 8:33 *allows* another antecedent. This article contends that it *expects* another one.

[14] John himself *twice* (not the people themselves) calls them *believers* (8:30-31). Did John lie, as Calvin, *John 1–10*, 220, suggests? "…the Evangelist imprecisely calls [this in 8:30] faith…"

[15] R. C. H. Lenski, *The Interpretation of St. John's Gospel*, CNT (Columbus, OH: Wartburg, 1942), 632; Charles C. Bing, "The Condition for Salvation in John's Gospel," *JOTGES* 9 (Spring 1996), 36; Dillow, *Final Destiny*, 358.

[16] Hunn, "They," 398. Italics mine.

[17] Note *replied*, not *answered*. *Answer* implies: A asked B a question that B answered. *Reply* allows: A asked B a question; to which X replied. *Apekrithēsan* allows either *answer* or *reply*.

such a break. In 1992, comparing and contrasting 8:33 with vv 13, 19a, 22, 25a, 39a, 41b, 48, 52f, and 57 suggested to the author that John's Greek does signal such a transition.[18]

View three (a break between 8:32 and 8:33) can prove its point. However, Hendriksen's claim has an Achilles' heel. John 8:30-33's *very* words distinguish believers in 8:30-32 from the objectors in v 33, contrary to Hendriksen's supposition that 8:30-38 is, "...an uninterrupted story.... [without] transition from one group to another."[19]

V. TRANSITION BETWEEN JOHN 8:32 AND 8:33

John 8:30 says many believed. If these believers speak in v 33, it would be their *first* speech. John nearly always introduces new speakers via noun subjects.[20]

An example may clarify this point. Consider an editor proofreading the first page of a children's book. The scene is of a farmer's family conversation:

> Mr. Jones told his sons, "Get the cows for milking." Billy and Eddy said, "Sure, Dad." Then Billy challenged Eddy, "I'll find them before you." Soon, Eddy shouted, "I saw the cows first." "Let's go home," *they* said.

The editor spotted a confusing word: *they.* Readers might think Billy and Eddy (and maybe even Dad) said, "Let's go home." To whom does *they* refer?

The book's title is *Milly and Molly: Our Chatty Cattle* and is about talking cows. The text after this excerpt says that the cows actually spoke here. The proofreader recognized that changing "*they said*" to "*the cows said*" would assist readers. Consider the reworded paragraph, including the previously undisclosed section (especially the underlined part):

> Eddy shouted, "I saw the cows first." Milly and Molly, the cows, said, "Let's go home." Billy and Eddy just stared at each other. Billy

---

[18] Studying these texts in Greek, after having read Christianson, "*Pisteuō*," 182ff, who champions clearer (not nearer) antecedents, led quickly to formulating the argument explained in this article.

[19] Hendriksen, *John*, 2:50ff.

[20] Sections V and VI will establish this assertion.

said, "It can't be! <u>Did Milly and Molly really say what I think they said?</u>"

The reworded paragraph introduces Milly and Molly as speakers. Before they spoke, only humans in the book talked. A noun subject ("the *cows* said") is clearer than a pronoun (*they* said) here.[21]

Someone may object: "The example is apples and oranges. No one thinks that cows *can* talk, but everyone knows that people can." That misses the point. Yes, they possess the ability to speak, but *would* they dare to do so in 8:33? Jerusalem's powerful religious leaders sought to intimidate Jesus and many of his followers. Who imagines that baby believers would stick their necks out to interrupt? If that were actually the case, John would have written, "Those believers answered..." The talking cows illustration is fitting.

John 8:33 lacks a noun subject. The verse does not suggest any new speakers entering the fray. It is just the same old hecklers speaking again.

A. Third Person Verbs Introducing/ Re-Introducing Speakers (3VIRIS)

John strongly prefers explicit noun subjects for new speakers, not implicit (or even explicit) pronouns. All seven times the Samaritan woman speaks (4:9, 11, 15, 17, 19, 25, and 28), *woman* is the subject. John 4 never says *she said*. This article's thesis is that John strongly prefers noun-subjects for speaking verbs, especially when introducing *new* speakers.

B. A Conversation Similar to John 8

Imagine another conversation like this:

Jim was teaching John 1:1 to his sons, Bob and Ed, at home. They absorbed it all. The doorbell rang. Jehovah's Witnesses were at the door and said, "Hi, we are Bible students." Jim turned to Bob and Ed, saying, "Later, we will resume John 1:1 which calls Jesus eternal-God, part of the Trinity." *They responded,* "How can you call Jesus the eternal God? He is a creature. The Trinity is nonsense."

---

[21] Stephen H. Levinsohn, *Discourse Features of New Testament Greek*, 2nd ed. (Dallas, TX: SIL International, 2000), 134-47 has useful background information for this section of the article.

Who would claim that *they responded* refers to Bob and Ed, who "absorbed it all" about Jesus and the Trinity from John 1:1? *They* refers to the door-knockers. John 8:20-33's structure resembles that of the story of Jim:

> 20 Jesus said these sayings in the treasury, while teaching...
> 22 Then [heckling] Judeans again said...
> 28 Then Jesus told them...
> 31 Then Jesus told the Judeans who believed Him...
> 33 "We are Abraham's seed," they replied to Him...

John 8:20 (not 8:30) is the start of the section. Both teachable crowds and hecklers were there. John 8 has a structure similar to the story of Jim and his sons.

Hendriksen is oblivious to the presence of receptive hearers who were learning as Jesus taught (8:20). One must remember that teaching has as its goal "causing someone to learn something." The extent of what Hendriksen says regarding *teaching* (as he comments on 8:20) is, "Here Jesus was teaching..."[22] Did he not realize that "Jesus was teaching" implies "people were learning"? He imagines everyone there (besides the Twelve) as hostile to Jesus. Hendriksen was blind—not expecting the presence of teachable people there—many of whom would come to faith.

The first draft of the talking-cows story was poorly written. It tried to introduce new speakers (Milly and Molly the cows) with *they said*. The book's second draft announced the first speech by cows with: "The *cows* said..."

John's Gospel employs good writing style. Nearly always John introduces new speakers via noun subjects. If Hendriksen were right about there being no break between 8:32 and 8:33, John would have said, "These believers said..." Failing that, 8:33 re-introduces the hecklers who already spoke in 8:13, 19a, 22, 25a. They again object in 39a, 41b, 48, 52-53, and 57.

Similarly, in the story about Jim, the sons have no speaking role. *They responded* should refer to prior speakers, the door-knockers. Unlike the sons, the visitors did speak. The word "they" naturally

---

[22] Hendriksen, *John*, 2:44.

refers to them. Like Bob and Ed, the new believers in John 8:30-32 have no speaking role. They are silent.

This hypothesis needs to be tested. The focus will be upon how John introduces new speakers versus how he reintroduces old ones.

VI. PROVING A BREAK BETWEEN JOHN 8:32 AND 33

A three-pronged investigation will show that the speakers in 8:33 are not the believers of 8:30-32. It will look, first of all, at John's use of third person verbs introducing/re-introducing speakers (hereafter 3VIRIS).[23] Secondly, it will consider how John uses 3VIRIS with and without explicit subjects (3VIRIS w/S versus 3 VIRIS w/o S). Finally, it will consider how frequently 3VIRIS w/o S do or do not re-introduce old speakers.

How John handles the speakers in 8:33 follows his pattern for re-introducing old speakers. His style reveals a break in 8:32 and 8:33 that Hendriksen missed.

A. 3VIRIS in John's Gospel

John's Gospel in the *Majority Text* has 3,669 verbs. Only 353 verbs[24] (10%) involve third person verbs of speaking, such as *say, speak, ask, answer, testify, shout,* etc., that involve contemporary speakers. Such verbs may appear for a character's first, second, or tenth time speaking.

The 353 3VIRIS in John uses introduce or re-introduce contemporary[25] speakers. Examples include: *Jesus said…, Judeans asked…, John [the Baptist] testified…, the woman asked…,* etc. Thus, one subject with two verbs (e.g., *Jesus answered and said*) or one verb with two subjects (*Philip and Andrew said*) count only once.

---

[23] First and second person verbs are not pertinent to this study.

[24] The Appendix lists the 353 3VIRIS verbs references.

[25] Third person speaking verbs not introducing contemporary speakers were excluded from the 353. These are of two types: (1) Some quote OT passages, such as "Isaiah said…" (cf. John 1:23; 12:39, 41) (2) Others use negated 3VIRIS verbs to deny that anyone said this or that. John 4:27 says, "No one said, 'Why…?'" Cf. 21:12. These are *non-speakers.*

B. 3VIRIS w/ S Versus 3VIRIS w/o S Verbs in John's Gospel

How does John handle subjects for the 353 3VIRIS verbs? Three options exist for Greek 3VIRIS verbs:

> 1. Noun + 3VIRIS: *Andres apekrithēsan*: "men replied" [3VIRIS w/ S].
> 2. Pronoun + 3VIRIS: *Autoi apekrithēsan*: "they replied" [3VIRIS w/ S].
> 3. [3VIRIS w/o S]: *Apekrithēsan*: "they replied."

By contrast, English 3VIRIS verbs must have explicit subjects. (Numbers two and three above translate identically: "they replied"). Readers may not know that Greek allows option three (i.e., the verb's subject is found in its pronoun ending, not in a separate and explicitly stated subject), since English verbs do not have pronoun endings and thus *must* have explicitly stated subjects.

C. How Many 3VIRIS w/o S Verbs in John Re-Introduce Old Speakers?

Only seventy-nine of John's Gospel's 353 3VIRIS verbs (22%) lack explicit subject words (3VIRIS w/o S).[26] John 8:33 employs a 3VIRIS w/o S.[27] Is this how John introduces new speakers? Those who already heckled Jesus (8:13, 19a, 22, 25a, 33, 39a, 41b, 48, 52f, and 57) would be old speakers; those who believed in 8:30 would be new ones—if they had spoken.

---

[26] John's 353 3VIRIS, 274 3VIRIS w/ S, and 79 3VIRIS w/o S references appear in the Appendix.

[27] The Greek says *apekrithēsan*, not *autoi apekrithēsan*. Both mean, "They replied," but excluding *autoi* signals an unemphatic subject. Most translations wrongly suggest an emphatic "they" by putting it first in v 33. Read the two renderings below. Both mean the same thing, but *they* only receives emphasis in the first (because it is the first word). The latter reflects John's Greek:

"*They* replied to Him, "We are Abraham's seed" (emphatic *they*).

"We are Abraham's seed," they replied to Him" (unemphatic *they*).

The 1996 translation by Arthur L. Farstad, "The Gospel of John—Logos 21 Version," which appears in *Living Water: The Gospel of John* (Glide, OR: Absolutely Free, 1996), renders John 8:33a, "'We are descendants of Abraham,' they answered Him…" Farstad insightfully moves the clause with *they* after beginning the quotation. My translation follows his lead on this issue.

Only between eight and ten of seventy-nine (10–13%) 3VIRIS w/o S introduce new speakers. Also, *none* occur in the midst of heckling. Almost all 3VIRIS w/o S verbs re-introduce old speakers (87–90%), and that is the case 100% of the time in heckling contexts. This is of utmost importance, because 8:33 uses a 3VIRIS w/o S verb in the midst of heckling.

VII. CONSIDERING JOHN 8:33

In 8:31-32 Jesus addresses the new "believers" of 8:30. In 8:33 it says that "they replied." In answering the question as to who the "they" are, it is important that the verb "replied" is a 3VIRIS w/o S verb.

Teachable people were in the crowd, because the concept of teaching (8:20) carries with it the idea, or the goal of, "causing someone to learn something." Many, such as Hendriksen, lose sight of the elephant in the room, i.e., the receptive crowds.[28] But objectors were also there (8:13-19). Two contrasting groups heard Jesus simultaneously. His positive teaching (8:12, 31-32) addresses receptive believers. His rebuttals rebuke the hecklers. Totally wrong-headed is Hendriksen's claim that 8:30-38 is "...an uninterrupted story.... [without] transition from one group to another."[29] Rather, a break exists between 8:32 and 8:33.

John's use of a 3VIRIS w/o S verb ("they replied") refers to hecklers opposing Jesus in 8:33. The new believers did not suddenly join the opposition.

A break appears between 8:32 and 8:33, facilitating an evaluation of the three views discussed above in section III. View one, which holds that there is unity between 8:32 and 8:33 and that the believers of 8:30-32 are non-persevering believers, is wrong because it does not see the break between 8:32 and 8:33.

The remaining question is whether the passage requires perseverance for eternal life. This issue determines whether view two (perseverance is required) or view three (the believers of 8:30 are saved and have assurance) offers the correct approach to this passage.

---

[28] See critique of Hendriksen in section V, B above.

[29] Hendriksen, *John*, 2:50*ff*.

VIII. JOHN 8:30-32: FAITH, NOT PERSEVERANCE, RESULTS IN ETERNAL LIFE

Views one and two both require final perseverance for eternal life. This denies assurance of eternal life while in a mortal body.

John's Gospel teaches that at the point of faith, one has eternal life and knows it. John 3:16; 5:24; 6:47, etc., prove that everlasting life comes at the moment of belief. John 4:10 calls eternal life God's *gift*, not merely a good deal. John 1:12 says that ones who believe in His name become God's children. John 5:24 states that believers (while on earth) pass from death to life; therefore, they will go to neither the Great White Throne nor the lake of fire. All believers already possess, by faith, everlasting life.

Jesus urged new believers to "abide" in His word. If they did so, they would truly be His "disciples" (v 31) and would be "free" (v 32). This is a message for believers. Believing differs from discipleship. Disciples follow in Christ's word by doing what He teaches, following in His footsteps.

"Abiding" in Jesus' word does not equal believing in Him for eternal life. Long before John 13–17, the Eleven had believed His promise of everlasting life by faith in Him. Jesus urged that group of believers to *abide*:

> If you abide in Me and My words abide in you, you will ask whatever you wish, and it shall come to be for you. My Father is glorified by this: that you may bear much fruit; and you will become[30] My disciples. Just as the Father has loved Me, I also have loved you; abide in My love. If you keep My commandments, you will abide in My love, just as I have kept My Father's commandments and abide in His love (John 15:7-10).

This concept closely matches that of John 8:30-32. Both times Jesus exhorts *believers* to walk in His footsteps, abide in His word, spend time with Him, learn more of Him, and become His disciples.

---

[30] Note *become* (*ginomai*, not *eimi*). Despite having believed, the Eleven still needed to become disciples. This same issue appears in 15:7-10. Thomas particularly struggled, because he was not present in 20:19-23. Not being with Jesus then caused him grief. In John 15:7-10, the Eleven, although already believers, still needed to become disciples.

IX. CONCLUSION

This article deals extensively with grammar. Knowing how John uses 3VIRIS w/o S verbs clarifies 8:30-33.

In reality, though, this article is not primarily grammatical. It shows that John 8:31-32 explains glorious discipleship prospects for Christians. Believers already have eternal life, so worrying if one is a "real" believer is inappropriate. Instead, Jesus urges following in His footsteps. Abiding in His word as His disciples frees believers from walking in darkness. It also enables them to walk in the light of His word. Eternal life requires faith alone in Jesus Christ alone for His promise, not perseverance in good works. Assurance rests upon His certain promise to all believers. It is the basis for abiding (persevering) as disciples.

APPENDIX: JOHN'S 353 3VIRIS VERBS

John's Gospel has 353 3VIRIS verbs. Five references (2:9f; 4:41f; 8:3f; 12:12f; and 19:f) have one 3VIRIS extending into the next verse (marked by f). Others have more than one (labeled by a, b, and/or c after the reference). Verses lacking a, b, c, or f have only one 3VIRIS. These reflect the Hodges-Farstad, Majority Text, 2nd ed.

274 3VIRIS w/ S citations are not underlined.
+ 79 3VIRIS w/o S citations are not underlined.
353 3VIRIS citations in John's Gospel.

8 3VIRIS w/o S citations have n (n = new speaker introduced)
2 3VIRIS w/o S citations have e (e = either new speaker or old speaker)
+ 69 3VIRIS w/o S citations lack n or e (= old speaker re-introduced)
79 3VIRIS citations in John's Gospel.

1:15, 19n, 20n, 21abc, 22-23, 25n, 26, 29, 32, 36, 38ab, 39, 41-43, 45, 46ab, 47, 48ab, 49-50, 51; 2:3-5, 7, 8, 9f, 16, 18-20; 3:2-5, 9-10, 26, 27; 4:7, 9-11, 13, 15-16, 17ab, 19, 21, 25-26, 28, 31-34, 39, 41f, 48-51, 52; 5:6-8, 10, 11-12, 14, 17, 19; 6:5, 7-8, 10, 12, 14, 20, 25n, 26, 28, 29, 30, 32, 34, 35, 41, 42, 43, 52-53, 60-61, 65, 67-68, 70; 7:3, 6, 11, 12ab, 15-16, 20-21, 25, 28, 31, 33, 35, 37, 40, 41ab, 45-47, 50, 52; 8:3f, 7, 10, 11ab, 12-14, 19a, 19b, 21-22, 23, 25a, 25b, 28, 31, 33, 34, 39a, 39b, 41, 42, 48-49,

52, 54, 57-58; 9:2-3, 7, 8, 9a, 9bc, 10, 11, 12ab, 15, 16ab, 17a,
17b, 19, 20, 24, 25, 26, 28, 30, 34, 35-41; 10:7, 20-21, 24-25,
32-34, 41; 11:3-4, 7, 8-9, 11, 12, 14, 16, 21, 23, 24-25, 27-28,
31-32, 34ab, 36-37, 39ab, 40-41, 43, 44, 47, 49, 56e; 12:7, 12f,
19, 21, 23, 28, 29ab, 30, 34-35, 44; 13:6-7, 8ab, 9-10, 12, 21,
25-27, 31, 36ab, 37-38; 14:5-6, 8-9, 22-23; 16:17, 18, 19, 29, 31;
17:1; 18:4, 5an, 5b, 7a, 7b, 8, 11, 17ab, 20, 22-23, 25a, 25b, 26,
29, 30, 31ab, 33-36, 37ab, 38a, 38b, 40; 19:3n, 4, 5, 6ab, 7, 8f,
10-12, 14, 15abc, 21-22, 24e, 26, 27, 28, 30; 20:2n, 13a, 13bn,
15ab, 16ab, 17, 19, 21, 22, 25-26, 27, 28-29; 21:3a, 3b, 5a, 5b,
6-7, 10, 12, 15a, 15bc, 16abc, 17abc, 19, 21-22.

The seventy-nine 3VIRIS w/o S citations (following) appear by themselves:

1:19n, 20n, 21abc, 22-23, 25n, 29, 36, 39, 51; 2:8, 16; 3:26; 4:52;
5:11-12; 6:12, 25, 28, 30, 34, 42, 65, 70; 7:52; 8:7, 19a, 23, 25a,
33, 39a, 41; 9:7, 10, 12ab, 17a, 19, 24, 26, 28, 34; 11:7, 11, 27-28,
34ab, 43, 56e; 13:12; 16:18; 18:5an, 7a, 25b, 30, 38b; 19:3n, 5,
14, 24e, 27; 20:2n, 13bn, 22, 27; 21:3b, 5b, 15bc, 16abc, 17abc,
19.

The following lists the eight (8) 3VIRIS w/o S which refer to new speakers and two (2) that could refer to either old or new speakers. Note two issues: 1) 3VIRIS w/o S do not appear in heckler contexts, and 2) these ten references (of 79 3VIRIS w/o S) are only 13% of the uses (8 of 79 = 10%). Thus, 87–90% of John's uses of the 3VIRIS w/o S category are reintroductions of old speakers. That is John's strong default, so one needs a compelling reason for assigning any 3VIRIS w/o S to the "new speaker introduced" category.

1:19n, 20n, 25n; 6:25n; 11:56e; 18:5an; 19:3n, 24e; 20:2n, 13bn.

Message of Life's website has a more detailed presentation of these passages concerning 3VIRIS verbs. It lists both the verb and its subject or (in cases of 3VIRIS w/o S) an explicit subject's absence (www. MOL316.com).

A CLOUDY VIEW OF SALVATION: DAVID W. CLOUD ON REPENTANCE

SHAWN LAZAR

Associate Editor

I. INTRODUCTION

David W. Cloud is a Fundamental Baptist missionary, writer, and publisher. His *Way of Life Literature* is well-known in Fundamentalist circles and defends many conservative positions with which readers of *JOTGES* would agree. Cloud has even explicitly written against Lordship Salvation. But how consistent is he in rejecting it?

II. FREE GRACE FRIENDLY POSITIONS

Cloud takes several positions that would naturally align him with Free Grace Theology. In this section, I list six such positions.

A. Cloud Is a Dispensationalist

In an article entitled, "Study the Bible Dispensationally,"[1] Cloud affirms that a "consistent application of the literal method of interpretation will result in a dispensational theology."[2] He warns against Covenant Theology, Progressive Dispensationalism, and Hyper-Dispensationalism. Cloud seems to favor Dispensationalism as taught by Scofield and Charles Ryrie without requiring complete adherence to any one system.[3]

B. Cloud Affirms Faith Alone

Cloud affirms that we are saved by faith alone, not by works. For example, in the *Way of Life Encyclopedia of the Bible & Christianity*,

---

[1] https://www.wayoflife.org/database/study_bible_dispensationally.html.
[2] Ibid.
[3] Ibid.

Cloud writes: "Salvation is through faith ALONE and grace ALONE, not by any mixture of grace and law, faith and works (Ro. 4:13-16; 11:6)."[4] It is difficult to miss the emphasis on "alone." Cloud then writes a paragraph with which many *JOTGES* readers would agree:

> Faith alone is the door into God's wonderful salvation. Having been forgiven and blessed with eternal blessings in Christ, we serve God with a thankful heart—not in order to be saved or in order to perfect our salvation, but because we have been saved. We are not saved by works; we are saved unto works (Ep. 2:8-10; Titus 3:4-8).[5]

Again, we see the emphasis on "faith alone." And Cloud is intent on clarifying that we do good works because *we have been* saved by faith alone, not *to be* saved. This is strongly in keeping with Free Grace Theology. However, as we will see in later sections, Cloud contradicts himself on this point.

C. Cloud Defends Easy Believism in Principle

Cloud offers *qualified* support for "easy believism." Many people reject the term outright. Not Cloud. He defends—at least in principle—the idea that salvation is both easy and by believing:

> There is an evangelistic methodology in Christian circles today which is a plague to sound gospel preaching. Some call this "easy believism," but I don't like that term. *Belief is exactly what God requires for salvation.* "For by grace are ye saved *through faith*; and that not of yourselves: it is the gift of God: Not of works, lest any man should boast" (Eph. 2:8-9). "For God so loved the world, that he gave his only begotten Son, that *whosoever believeth* in him should not perish, but have everlasting life" (Jn. 3:16). Salvation is received by believing. Further, *God has made it easy to do.* A child can trust Christ and be saved; a weak-minded person can trust Christ and be saved. Salvation is not difficult, except in the sense that the sinner has to humble himself and repent (emphasis his).[6]

---

[4] Emphasis his. David W. Cloud, *Way of Life Encyclopedia of the Bible & Christianity*, 6th ed. (Port Huron, MI: Way of Life Literature, 2016), 573.

[5] Ibid.

[6] David W. Cloud, "Repentance and Lordship Salvation Revisited." See https://www.wayoflife.org/database/repentancerevisited.html. Accessed Oct. 29, 2018.

The real problem, Cloud believes, is not easy believism per se, but what he calls "quick prayerism." This is the method of evangelism that claims someone has been saved after saying a sinner's prayer.[7]

D. Cloud Affirms Eternal Security

Cloud believes in eternal security. For example, in his *Believer's Bible Dictionary*, he defends the eternality of salvation, using arguments that will be familiar to Free Grace advocates:

> *How can we be sure that the believer is eternally secure?* (1) Because of the terms used to describe salvation: "eternal life" (Jn. 3:16; 1 Jn 5:11); "full assurance" (Heb. 6:11; Col. 2:2); "strong consolation" (Heb. 6:18); "hope...sure and steadfast" (Heb. 6:19).[8]

> How do we know these blessings cannot be lost? (1) The blessings of salvation cannot be lost because of the nature of salvation: Salvation is eternal (Jn. 3:16, 36); salvation is a present possession (Ro. 5:1; 1 Pe. 2:24-25); salvation is by imputation and substitution (Ep. 1:3 "in Christ"; Ro. 6:7; Col. 2:10; 3:1-4, 12); salvation is not of human merit; it is a free gift of grace which cannot be mixed with works...[9]

Cloud believes that eternal security is part of the very meaning of life being "eternal." Note especially the last sentence in which Cloud affirms that salvation is a free gift "which cannot be mixed with works." This is consistent with his insistence that salvation is by faith "alone," that is, that it excludes works.

E. Cloud Distinguishes Between Relationship and Fellowship

Cloud distinguishes between a believer's eternal *relationship* with God and his conditional *fellowship* with God. For example, in commenting on 1 John, he explains,

> Here the Lord makes a plain distinction between relationship and fellowship. The theme of 1 John is found in 1:3. The theme

---

[7] Ibid.; cf. David Cloud, *The Hyles Effect: A Spreading Blight* (Port Huron, MI: Way of Life, 2014), 75.

[8] David W. Cloud, *Believer's Bible Dictionary* (Port Huron, MI: Way of Life, 2015), 93.

[9] Ibid., 94

is fellowship, not relationship. It is written to those who have established a relationship with God as children through faith in Christ.[10]

Your relationship with God is established through faith. But fellowship is established on other conditions. Cloud sees this distinction also taught in John's Gospel:

> In John 1-12 the focus is on the unsaved and the main message is "believe on the Lord Jesus Christ" (Jn. 1:7, 12; 3:15-16, 18; 4:39; 5:24; 6:35, 47; 7:38; 8:24; 9:35; 10:38; 11:26). When the unsaved asked about doing the works of God, Christ replied, "This is the work of God, that ye believe on him whom he hath sent" (Jn. 6:29). Faith in Christ is the only work God will accept from the unsaved.[11]

Notice that Cloud takes John 6:29 as Jesus teaching that faith, not works, is necessary for salvation. That is the only requirement from the unsaved. Free Grace advocates would heartily agree.

Cloud goes on to notice a change in the theme of John's Gospel when Jesus begins to teach in the Upper Room:

> This change in theme of John's Gospel illustrates the difference between relationship and fellowship. Faith is the requirement for eternal relationship; obedience is the requirement for daily fellowship. Faith is the way to become a child of God; obedience is the way to walk in fellowship with the Father.[12]

While the relationship is by faith alone, the fellowship is by obedience. Once again, Free Grace advocates would strongly agree with this theological distinction. Knowing the difference between our position and our condition is key to avoiding the danger of Lordship Salvation and to putting works in their proper doctrinal "place."

F. Cloud Rejects Both Calvinism and Arminianism

Cloud rejects both Calvinism and Arminianism. He explains why he rejects Calvinism in his book *The Calvinism Debate*.[13] To summarize: "If isolated and interpreted through Calvinistic lenses, there

---

[10] Cloud, *Encyclopedia*, 574.
[11] Ibid.
[12] Ibid.
[13] David W. Cloud, *The Calvinism Debate* (Port Huron, MI: Way of Life Literature, 2006, 2013).

are verses that seem to teach Calvinism, but when Scripture is taken as a whole it crumbles."[14] He does not see it established by Scripture.

However, that does not mean Cloud identifies as an Arminian. In fact, he explicitly rejects both Calvinism and Arminianism:

> James White, author of "The Truth about the King James Bible Controversy" and "The Potter's Freedom" and several other books, wrote to me in about the year 1999 and challenged me to a public debate. He urged me to "defend Arminianism." That is a strange notion, I don't follow Arminianism and I don't care anything about Arminianism. I have studied the theology of James Arminius some and I find errors in it just as I have found errors in John Calvin's theology. Though I do believe that Arminius was closer to the truth than Calvin, this does not mean that I have any intention to "defend Arminianism." White has the idea that is so typical among Calvinists that if a man is not a Calvinist, he is surely an Arminian.[15]

Hence, without giving a name for his theology, Cloud does not consider himself either a Calvinist or an Arminian.

G. Summary

All of these positions would seem to put Cloud close to the Free Grace camp. His Dispensationalism, emphasis on faith alone, the conditional nature of spiritual maturity, the possibility of carnality, and the doctrine of eternal security and rejection of both Calvinism and Arminianism would make it seem he is very Free Grace-friendly. That impression is made all the stronger by Cloud's explicit rejection of Lordship Salvation.

---

[14] Ibid., 15.
[15] Ibid., 12.

III. CLOUD REJECTS LORDSHIP SALVATION

David Cloud rejects Lordship Salvation by name in two articles, "Repentance and Lordship Salvation,"[16] and "Repentance and Lordship Salvation Revisited."[17] Those articles show he is aware that Lordship Salvation amounts to a gospel of works salvation.

A. Lordship Salvation Is Salvation by Works

We saw that Cloud affirms that salvation is by faith "alone." It comes as little surprise, then, that Cloud understands that the evangelistic demand to make Christ Lord of your life is a covert form of salvation by works:

> We do not support any idea of "Lordship Salvation" that teaches that an individual must make Jesus Christ Lord of every area of his life before he can be saved. Salvation does not produce perfect obedience nor does it require perfect understanding of theology. A genuinely born again Christian can be carnal. The Bible plainly teaches this (1 Corinthians 3).
>
> To require that a sinner make Jesus Christ Lord of every area of his life is an impossibility and would be the greatest form of works salvation ever devised. This false doctrine is taught by some independent Baptists, but we do not support it. It is a very dangerous doctrine that causes people to look inside themselves and to examine their experience rather than to look solely upon the Lord Jesus Christ and to trust solely upon His shed blood.[18]

Cloud makes several excellent statements in these two paragraphs. For example, *JOTGES* readers will appreciate how Cloud recognizes that some believers can be "carnal." That ties in with Cloud's teaching that fellowship with God is conditional. If you can be out of fellowship with God, you can be carnal.

Cloud is also correct to criticize turning inward, presumably to our works, for assurance of salvation, instead of looking "solely upon the Lord Jesus Christ." Indeed, the only object of saving faith and assurance is Jesus' promise of eternal life.

---

[16] David Cloud, "Repentance and Lordship Salvation." See https://www.wayoflife.org/database/repentance_lordship_salvation.html. Accessed Nov. 16, 2018.

[17] David Cloud, "Repentance Revisited." See https://www.wayoflife.org/database/repentancerevisited.html. Accessed Nov. 16, 2018.

[18] Cloud, "Repentance and Lordship Salvation."

However, notice that Cloud hedges his criticism of Lordship Salvation. He does not say that demanding *any* level of obedience to Christ for salvation is wrong. Although he denies supporting "any idea" of Lordship Salvation, he only rejects the claim that you must make Jesus Lord "of every area" of life, or that you must have "perfect obedience" to be saved. Does that mean you must make Jesus Lord of *some* areas of your life, or that you must have *some* level of obedience to Christ to be saved?

B. Lordship Salvation Confuses Justification and Sanctification

Cloud correctly recognizes the possibility that a born-again person can be carnal. He also draws a distinction between justification and sanctification, or between our standing and our state. As Cloud explains, confusing the two can lead to salvation by works:

> To preach a "lordship salvation" that requires that sinners make Jesus Christ absolute Lord of every area of their lives in order to be saved is to confuse position and practice, justification and sanctification. This is similar to the error made by many Pentecostals and Charismatics who believe the child of God can lose his salvation. An excellent testimony about the danger of this false teaching is in the book "Holiness: The False and the True" by the late Harry A. Ironside (Loizeaux).[19]

Although it is heartening to read Cloud reject Lordship Salvation, again, note Cloud's choice of language. He rejects the call to make Jesus "absolute" Lord of "every area" of life. Why add those qualifications? What about more modest Lordship claims? Would Cloud agree that Jesus must be the Lord of "some" areas of your life to be saved? Does that not also involve teaching salvation by works?

---

[19] Cloud, "Repentance and Lordship Salvation."

IV. CLOUD'S INCONSISTENT POSITION ON REPENTANCE

Unfortunately, Cloud's doctrine of salvation is inconsistent. Ultimately, despite denying Lordship Salvation, Cloud makes works a condition of salvation. For example, that is shown in his doctrine of repentance.

Earlier, we quoted Cloud explicitly saying that faith *alone* is the sole condition of salvation. Is Cloud consistent in that affirmation? It turns out he is not. He contradicts himself by heavily emphasizing that repentance is a condition for salvation.

A. What Repentance Is Not

In his article on "Biblical Repentance" and elsewhere, Cloud has explained what repentance is not. For example, it is not a synonym for faith: "Bible preachers proclaimed repentance, and if faith is the same as repentance as some claim, this would make no sense."[20]

Nor is it a mere change of mind. In his comments condemning what he calls "quick prayerism," Cloud thinks it is wrong to redefine repentance in that way. He says: "Quick Prayerism is an evangelistic methodology that is quick to get people to pray a sinner's prayer after a shallow gospel presentation and usually without any hint of the necessity of repentance (or redefining repentance to be the same as faith or to be a mere 'change of mind')."[21]

Cloud lists a number of other things that are not equivalent to repentance: it is more than remorse, confession, acknowledgment of sin, or changing from unbelief to belief.[22]

So what is repentance, according to Cloud?

B. Cloud's Definition of Repentance

According to Cloud, repentance is a change of mind that leads to a change of life:

---

[20] Cloud, *Bible Dictionary*, 273

[21] Cloud, *Hyles*, 75.

[22] David Cloud, "Biblical Repentance." See https://www.wayoflife.org/database/biblical_repentance.html. Accessed Nov. 16, 2018.

Biblical repentance as preached by John the Baptist, the Lord Jesus Christ, and the apostles, *is a change of mind toward God and sin that* results in *a change of life. It is a Spirit-wrought change of mind that leads to a change of life.* It is not a change of life. That would be works salvation. It is a radical, Spirit-wrought change of mind toward sin and God, such a dramatic change that it changes one's actions.[23]

Cloud emphasizes that genuine repentance *results in* a changed life:

It is not a change of life; it is a change of mind so radical that *it results in a change of life. It means to turn around and go in a different direction.* It means to lay down your arms and *to surrender to God*, to stop being at enmity against Him. I believe this is exactly what the Bible teaches about repentance, and I have shown this in the original article on Repentance, *but nowhere have I said that repentance means to repent of all your sin or to turn away from all of your sin. That would be a works salvation, which is a false gospel.*[24]

Here again, Cloud says that repentance is a change of mind that results in a radical change of life. And he again emphasizes the words "results in." Why? He adds "results in" because if repentance were itself *a changed life* involving works, and if repentance were a condition of salvation, "That would be works salvation."

You can also sense Cloud's hesitancy with his definition when he clarifies that the change is not so radical that it means you repent or turn away from "*all* your sin." He admits that, too, would be a "false gospel." Elsewhere he repeats: "Repentance is not turning from *all* sin in the sense of some sort of sinless perfection; it is a change of mind toward sin so that the sinner no longer intends to walk in rebellion against God."[25]

This definition creates a tension (or outright contradiction) in his theology. Cloud thinks he can avoid teaching works salvation if he qualifies his definition of repentance with the words "results in." If it only results in doing good works, but is not itself good works, then making repentance a condition of salvation may not be a form of salvation by works.

---

[23] Ibid.

[24] Cloud, "Repentance Revisited," emphasis added.

[25] Cloud, "Biblical Repentance," emphasis added.

Elsewhere Cloud says: "The fact that God *requires that we turn from sin* does not mean that salvation is by works. We know that the works are *the fruit of* genuine salvation, not *the cause of* it."[26] If Cloud consistently distinguished between repentance and the works that follow repentance, he could avoid the charge of works salvation. But, as he himself says, God requires that we turn from sin. If turning from sin is required, then it is a condition of salvation.

C. Repentance Means Doing Works

In the *Believer's Bible Dictionary*, Cloud gives several illustrations of what it means to repent. Notice his language. Cloud does not say that repentance results in works. He will say "Repentance is..." and then names a work:

> 1. Repentance is the Prodigal Son coming to right thinking, confessing his sin against God and his father, and returning home (Lk. 15:17-20).
> 2. Repentance is the Thessalonians turning to God from idols to serve the living and true God (1 Th. 1:9).
> 3. Repentance is Zacchaeus turning from corruption to uprightness (Lk. 19:8-9).
> 4. Repentance is Nebuchadnezzar humbling himself before God (Da. 4:37).
> 5. Repentance is the Philippian jailer turning to Jesus Christ and becoming a kind of helper of Christians (Acts 16:33-34).
> 6. Repentance is the Christ-rejecting Jews at Pentecost turning to Christ and continuing in obedience (Acts 2:38-42).[27]

In this list, Cloud explicitly identifies repentance with doing works. This contradicts those places where he tries to distinguish the two, such as: "To say that repentance results in works is not the same as saying that repentance is works."[28] So why, in the list above, does Cloud explicitly say that repentance "is" this or that work? His doctrine of repentance is inconsistent at this point. For Cloud, repentance is both a work and results in works.

---

[26] Ibid., emphasis added.

[27] Cloud, *Believer's Bible Dictionary*, 275.

[28] Cloud, "Biblical Repentance."

D. Repentance Is Necessary for Salvation

Cloud believes that repentance is necessary for salvation. This directly contradicts his claims that salvation is by faith *alone*. Salvation cannot be by faith alone if it is also by repentance. So what does Cloud believe—is salvation by faith alone, or by faith plus repentance that results in a changed life? You can cite passages for both ideas. We already quoted Cloud defending faith alone. But here he criticizes evangelism that does not mention the co-condition of repentance: "The typical soul-winning plan doesn't even hint at repentance, that there is going to be a change of direction, a submission to God."[29]

Why would that be a problem? Because according to Cloud, without repentance, there is no salvation:

> Salvation demands repentance (Lk 13:3-5; Ac. 2:38-42; 17:30-31). Repentance means a change of mind resulting in a change of life (2 Cor. 7:8-11). The person who has never changed his mind about God, sin, Christ, the Bible, etc., and who has never shown evidence of this in his life, has never repented and is not saved.[30]

Clearly, there is a contradiction in this theology.

Likewise, recall that when Cloud defended easy believism, he qualified his statement with these words: "Salvation is not difficult, *except in the sense that the sinner has to humble himself and repent*."[31] Repentance is here made part of the condition of salvation (does that

---

[29] Cloud, *Calvinism*, 52. By contrast, the Gospel of John, the only self-described evangelistic book in the Bible, does not mention repentance. Neither do the Books of Romans or Galatians.

[30] Cloud, *Dictionary*, 94. But I disagree that his proof-texts show that repentance is necessary to be born again. Luke 13:3-5 and Acts 2:38-42 are about being saved from the temporal judgment of AD 70, not about being born again. If you want to avoid the natural and divine consequences of sin in this life, you must repent of them. If you want to avoid dying of a drug overdose, you should repent of taking drugs. If you want to avoid divorce, repent of adultery. If you want to avoid being shot to death, repent of robbing stores. Temporal salvation does depend on repentance. But that does not prove you must repent in order to be born again. If eternal salvation demands repentance, how much repentance must you do and for how long before you are born again? Making behavior change a condition of salvation obscures the truth that salvation happens in a moment, through a single act of faith in Christ for eternal life, totally apart from works. Careful readers should consider whether Cloud's proof-texts address eternal salvation, or some other type of deliverance.

[31] Cloud, "Repentance and Lordship Salvation Revisited," emphasis added.

make humbling yourself a third co-condition for salvation or one of the works of repentance?). And Cloud implies it is difficult, in the sense you must be humbled and repent.

Indeed, Cloud says that salvation itself is described as coming to repentance:

> Salvation is referred to as coming to repentance with no mention of faith in Matthew 9:13; 11:20-21; 21:32; Mark 1:4; 2:17; 6:12; Luke 15:7; 24:47; Acts 2:38; 3:19; 5:31; 11:18; 26:20; 2 Corinthians 7:10; 1 Thessalonians 1:9; 2 Timothy 2:25; and 2 Peter 3:9.[32]

E. Why This Ends in Denying Faith Alone

Does Cloud evade the charge of denying salvation by faith alone? No, he does not.

First, if salvation is by faith plus repentance, and repentance is not a synonym for faith, then salvation is not by faith alone. It is by faith plus repentance. Cloud contradicts himself.

Second, if you are only saved by repentance that results in works, and not by one without works, then your salvation depends upon works. Cloud is aware of that implication and seeks to avoid the charge of teaching salvation by works by saying, "nowhere have I said that repentance means to repent of all your sin or to turn away from all of your sin. That would be a works salvation, which is a false gospel."[33] He seems to think that so long as you do not require repentance from *all* sins, you avoid works salvation. But according to the Apostle Paul, adding *any* amount of works to the saving message turns it into another gospel (Gal 1:6-9). In other words, requiring

---

[32] David W. Cloud, "Why Doesn't John 3:16 and Acts 16:31 Mention Repentance?" See https://www.wayoflife.org/database/john316repentance.html. Accessed Oct. 29, 2018. Readers ought to look up each of those passages and ask what kind of salvation is discussed in each passage (e.g., is it earthly or eternal?). While it is true that repentance featured prominently in Jesus' preaching and in NT teaching, that is not enough to show it is a co-condition for being born again. What is repentance for? Is it for Israel to receive the kingdom? Is it preparatory to faith? Is it for restoration of fellowship with God? Is it to avoid temporal discipline and destruction? Simply quoting verses that have the word *repentance* does not show that it is a synonym for faith, part of faith, or a condition for being born again.

[33] Cloud, "Repentance Revisited."

people to repent of *any amount of sin* as a condition of salvation would be works salvation. Even though Cloud does not require repentance from *all sin*, he does require repentance from *some*.[34] Hence, he teaches salvation by works.

V. THE DIFFERENCE BETWEEN FALSE FAITH AND GENUINE FAITH

Cloud's view of the relationship between salvation, faith, and repentance is involved in another contradiction. On the one hand, as we have seen, he strongly distinguishes between faith and repentance. However, there are other places where he explicitly redefines faith to include repentance within it. That is seen in his distinction between false faith and saving faith.

A. True Faith Includes Repentance

Cloud is evidently aware of Free Grace claims that it is significant that the only self-identified evangelistic book in the Bible, the Gospel of John, omits the word *repentance*: "Some men say that it is not necessary to preach repentance since we don't see it in John 3:16 and Acts 16:31…"[35] However, Cloud is not persuaded. Why not? Because he believes repentance is implied in the very concept of saving faith itself:

> The reason why verses such as John 3:16 and Acts 16:31 don't mention repentance is that proper saving faith includes repentance and proper repentance includes faith…By comparing Scripture with Scripture (rather than isolating Scripture, which is the method used by false teachers), I conclude that saving faith includes repentance. [36]

Repentance is implied in the concept of faith, but Cloud earlier denied that it is a synonym for faith. Redefining faith to include repentance that results in a changed life compromises the doctrine of justification at the root. It smuggles works into the definition of

---

[34] Of course, this also makes assurance of salvation impossible. How could anyone possibly know if he had turned from enough sins to be born again? He cannot.

[35] Cloud, "Why Doesn't John 3:16 and Acts 16:31 Mention Repentance?"

[36] Ibid.

faith itself. But if repentance is not a synonym for faith, why does Cloud think it is implied by the concept of faith? This is another contradiction.

B. Saving Faith Produces Good Works

Cloud says that saving faith produces good works. If it does not, it is not saving: "(4) Saving faith always produces good works (Ep 2:8-10; He 11:4, 7, 8; Ja 2:14-26). If a person claims to have faith in Christ, but his life does not reflect the works of Christ, that person does not have saving faith."[37]

Here is more evidence that Cloud teaches salvation by works. If you are only saved by a faith that produces good works, and not saved by faith that does not produce good works, then works are part of the condition of salvation. This is another form of salvation by works. It denies that we are saved by faith alone. That is a contradiction in Cloud's theology.

VI. CONCLUSION

There is much to admire in David Cloud's theology. This writer has benefited from his books and articles. Cloud takes several very strong positions for salvation by faith alone and against Lordship Salvation. Sadly, he then contradicts those positions with his doctrines of repentance and faith, both of which make salvation depend upon changing your behavior and doing good works. Cloud's soteriology is inconsistent. He ought to resolve the inconsistency by affirming faith alone—period. He should go back to his distinction between relationship and fellowship and see that repentance is a fellowship issue, not a relationship one.[38] In sum, Cloud should repent of his view of repentance.

---

[37] Cloud, *Bible Dictionary*, 94-95.

[38] See Zane C. Hodges, *Harmony with God: A Fresh Look at Repentance* (Dallas, TX: Redencion Viva, 2001).

Book Reviews

The Historical Reliability of the New Testament. By Craig Blomberg. Nashville, TN: B & H Academic, Lexham Press, 2016. 783 pp. Paper, $39.99.

Since my view of inerrancy is stricter than that of Blomberg, I began reading this book wondering if he would regularly question the historicity of the NT (i.e., would he say that it was historically reliable based on the standards of historiography when written, but it would not be historically reliable based on our current standards?). While his view on the Gospels is not totally to my liking, *The Historical Reliability of the New Testament* (THRNT) defends the historicity of the Gospels and the entire NT.

It is a mammoth book. However, despite its length, it really is not that hard of a read. For someone with a Th.B. or higher, I think THRNT will make perfect sense and will be relatively easy to follow. (For the layman this book may be heavy sledding, but it should still be readable.)

On the one hand, I was sorry to see Blomberg assert that the way to discern whether the Gospel writers and other ancient authors "erred in some of the statements they made" was "to have a feel for what would have counted as an error in the context in which the statement first appeared" (p. 26). He went so far as to say, "concluding that the Gospels are biographical is not the same as deciding that everything in them actually happened" (p. 27). My understanding of inerrancy is that the Bible is without error based on the highest standards of historiography.

On the other hand, I was pleased to see that with many of the discrepancies in the Gospel accounts, Blomberg suggests reasonable harmonizations (e.g., pp. 77, 78, 84, 85-86, 88-90, 95-96, 100-108). Unfortunately, he rules out (or finds highly unlikely) what he calls "classic additive harmonization" (p. 72) and "purely additive harmonization" (pp. 87-88). He is referring to those who would simply add together what different Gospel writers say. For example, some say (myself included) that the Father said both, "You are My beloved

Son" and "This is My beloved Son" at Jesus' baptism. Some think (myself included) that the centurion both sent representatives to Jesus and then later spoke with Him personally. In my opinion "additive harmonization" quite often tells us what actually happened.

While he seems to think it most likely that the cleansing of the temple in John 2 is "a topically or thematically relocated version of the incident" (p. 194), I was pleasantly surprised that Blomberg says that it is possible that the cleansing of the temple did occur twice, with the incident in John 2 occurring "in a comparatively small corner of the temple" (p. 195).

I appreciated the fact that Blomberg spoke of "apparent discrepancies" (pp. 50, 56, 71) and "seeming discrepancies" (p. 262).

In some cases THRNT finds the Gospel writers "recasting" (p. 74), "rewording" (p. 87), and "creating his own transliteration" (p. 75). It would have been nice if in cases where Blomberg could not come up with a harmonization which satisfied him, he would have affirmed the truthfulness of all the Gospel accounts and confessed that he has not yet come up with a harmonization, but that one certainly exists.

JOTGES readers will not be pleased with Blomberg's suggestion concerning John 8:30-32: "Even when believing seems to refer to an initial trust, in John it may not eventuate in abiding faith. Thus, classically, in 8:30, John writes that 'even as [Jesus] spoke, many believed in him.' But at least some in that same group of individuals are called children of the devil by verse 44, clarifying that it was not full-orbed saving faith John was originally describing" (p. 185).

Nor will they be satisfied with his suggestion that both Paul and James taught justification is by faith that works. He thinks that "Galatians 5:6 requires faith to be working through love, while Ephesians 2:10 follows immediately on the heels of salvation by grace through faith with the insistence that we are Christ's workmanship created for good works" (p. 507). Consistent with that view, he takes the *tests of life* understanding of 1 John (p. 508).

Amazingly, THRNT covers the entire NT, not just the Gospels. This book is a major reference work. If one wonders what the critics say about Acts, for example, and how we might respond, Blomberg gives excellent discussions. Every book receives attention.

(Blomberg also covers the Nag Hammadi literature and the New Testament Apocrypha [pp. 562-90].)

It was encouraging to see Blomberg say that "responsible scholarship does not find outside the New Testament enough reliable historical material to shed any substantially different light on the Jesus of history and his first followers" (p. 604).

Blomberg's treatment of textual criticism, though coming from a so-called *Critical Text perspective*, is fair and balanced, and it upholds the accuracy of the transmission of the text. In fact, he goes so far as to say, "We can say with a high degree of confidence that we have the actual text of the autographs of the New Testament" (p. 623). He clarifies that by adding that where there are textual variants, we have the original reading either in the text or in the footnotes (the apparatus that lists other variants). He says that the NT books were "copied with extraordinary care" (p. 659).

Blomberg ends the book with an excellent discussion of "The Problem of Miracles" (pp. 663-715). He does a great job of showing that if God exists, then the miraculous is no problem (p. 665). He gives "four classic arguments for his existence" (pp. 665-68). I especially liked his refutations of Hume's arguments (pp. 669-72). While I do not agree with his non-cessationist position (p. 677, note 34), I agree with him that God does miracles today. Here is a great comment, "There are no compelling scientific, philosophical, or 'comparative religions' reasons for approaching the New Testament miracles skeptically" (p. 685).

While I am to the right of Blomberg in my understanding of inerrancy, and while I disagree with some of what he has written in THRNT, I recommend this book. I think it is a valuable resource, well worth having.

Robert N. Wilkin
Associate Editor
Journal of the Grace Evangelical Society

Faith in Jesus: What Does It Mean to Believe in Him? By Edwin Aaron Ediger, ed. Roy B. Zuck. Bloomington, IN: WestBow Press, 2012. 430 pp. Paper, $30.95.

This is a tough book to review. On the one hand, Ediger does a great job of explaining and defending many Free Grace interpretations of tough texts. On the other hand, Ediger is confusing on the purported subject of the book, what it means to believe in Jesus.

You will find excellent discussion of verses like Matt 7:21-23; John 2:23-25; 8:30-32; 12:42-43; 2 Cor 13:5; and Jas 2:14-26.

However, Ediger attempts to disprove the idea of Gordon Clark and John Robbins that all faith is propositional (see pp. 3-24). Ediger sees some faith as believing a proposition and other faith, especially saving faith, as believing a proposition(s) and then trusting in a person (see pp. 13, 23-24, 409). He rejects the idea that "[saving] trust means to believe propositions to be true" (p. 8).

In at least one place he seems to contradict the idea that saving faith is both believing and trusting. He writes, "In salvific contexts it (believe) means *either* 'to believe something to be true' *or* 'to put one's trust in someone or something'" (p. 13, emphasis added). However, in other places he says the word *believe* "can include the thought of believing a proposition to be true and trusting in a person" (p. 54). It seems that the latter is his real view of saving faith, believing a proposition or propositions about the Person, work, and promise of Christ and then trusting in Him for one's eternal destiny (pp. 23-24). His point is that a person needs to believe enough propositional truth about Christ in order to then "place trust in that person for his eternal destiny" (p. 24).

On one occasion, when discussing the purpose statement of John's Gospel, John 20:31, Ediger says the first use of the word *believe* (believing that Jesus is the Christ, the Son of God) refers to believing propositions about Jesus and that the second use ("and that by believing you may have life in His name") refers to trusting in Him (pp. 218-19). He seems to imply here that any given use of the word *believe* carries one or the other meaning. But in light of the rest of the book, I doubt that is what he means. He seems to hold to the both/and view.

At one point Ediger implies that one must be fully Trinitarian and must believe everything that the Scriptures reveal about God the Father and God the Son to be born again. He writes, "Christological addition results in soteriological subtraction. To alter the biblical identification of either the Father or the Son means that eternal life is denied to the unsaved because it fundamentally changes the gospel" (p. 384). Surely he merely means that one must believe *the major truths* which Scripture reveals about the identity of the Father and the Son. To say that we must believe everything that is revealed would make regeneration impossible to achieve. But even saying that one must believe the major truths revealed about the Father and the Son makes it impossible for children to be born again (how can they believe in the virgin birth, the hypostatic union, the eternality of God, omniscience, omnipotence, etc.). In addition, it also makes salvation impossible for most adults. Certainly it would take weeks or months of study before a person would know enough about the Father and the Son to believe the major truths revealed in Scripture about them.

I find two significant problems which Ediger fails to solve. First, specifically which propositions must a person believe to be born again? He does not say, other than speaking favorably of J. B. Hixson's list of five essentials (pp. 7-8). But he never says that those five essentials cover all one must believe.

Second, what does it mean to trust in Jesus? If believing in Jesus for everlasting life (1 Tim 1:16) is not enough, then it is essential that we know what this second step is. What specifically must I do to trust in Christ? Ediger does not say. In some places he says that one must trust Him "for one's eternal destiny" (pp. 23, 24). However, in the last chapter, "The Biblical Gospel," Ediger talks about believing "the person and the provision," but does not mention the promise (p. 412). He says there, "Knowing about the person of Christ and the means of His provision, one is able to put his or her trust in Him" (p. 412). The very last line in the book is similarly ambiguous, "The task of evangelism is to present evidence about the person of Jesus and His provision of salvation and to invite them, even implore them, to put their trust in Him" (p. 413).

It is not clear whether Ediger believes that assurance is of the essence of saving faith. While he does say that one must "trust in [Him] for his eternal destiny" (p. 24), he does not indicate if this trust is certainty or is less than that (as when a dying man is told that he has a 50-50 chance of surviving the surgery and decides to trust the doctor as his only hope).

Finally, let me say a word about the nature of the twelve chapters in this book. The book is mostly a commentary. Nine of the twelve chapters walk through the Scriptures. This is especially evident in Chaps. 4-8, which are essentially short commentaries on Matthew,

Mark, Luke, John, and Acts. Ediger walks through each chapter in those five books, giving selective commentary. Presumably this commentary is showing what propositions about Jesus can lead us to trust Him for our eternal destiny. I think what he means is that one can be led to trust in Christ through many different propositions. But since he never says what the saving propositions are, the commentary chapters do not seem to go along with the other three chapters.

Ediger appears to be saying that prior to Jesus' baptism, people were born again by trusting in God the Father: "The Old Testament identifies God as the one in whom trust is to be placed, and prepares for the coming of the Messiah, identifying Him by prophetic means" (p. 65). Ediger later in the book specifically rejects the idea, for example, that Gen 15:6 refers to Abraham believing God's promise concerning the coming Messiah (p. 270).

The three chapters which give the most discussion of the book's title and subtitle are chaps. 1, 2, and 12. In chap. 1 he presents and rejects some of what Clark and Robbins said about propositional truth. Those of us who agree with Clark and Robbins would have liked to have seen a fairer presentation of their views. Chapter 2 looks at a few problem passages (Acts 2:38; Rom 10:9; 2 Cor 13:5). Chapter 12, the shortest in the book at just four and a half pages, tells us presumably what "The Biblical Gospel" is. Unfortunately, this is the chapter that needs the most discussion, not the least.

Ediger clearly rejects Lordship Salvation and works salvation. However, his presentation of the faith-alone message is not clear.

I would not recommend this book to new or untaught believers. However, I would recommend it for pastors, church leaders, and others who wish to stay abreast of the latest writings about saving faith by Free Grace people.

Robert N. Wilkin
Associate Editor
Journal of the Grace Evangelical Society

The Righteousness of God: The Heart of the Lutheran Reformation. By Don Matzat. O'Fallon, MO: Good News Books, 2017. 61 pp. Paper, $3.99.

Don Matzat is a Lutheran pastor and radio host. In this booklet, he explains the Lutheran doctrine of justification by faith apart from works.

In chap. 1, Matzat begins by giving a short account of how Martin Luther came to rediscover this doctrine. While historians celebrate Luther's nailing of the 95 Theses to the church door in Wittenberg as the start of the Reformation, Matzat claims Luther's Tower Experience was the pivotal moment in his life. "In his Tower Experience, Martin Luther uncovered the central New Testament teaching of justification by grace through faith because of Christ alone" (p. 11). Luther was meditating on Romans 1:17 when he finally came to believe that doctrine. Matzat quotes Luther: "Here I felt that I was altogether born again and had entered paradise itself though open gates" (p. 9).

In chap. 2 and 7, Matzat relates some sobering stories of how many Lutherans do not believe in justification by faith. Matzat tells how, after hearing that message, lifelong Lutherans have told him, "I never heard that before" (p. 15), or "All our pastors taught us we go to heaven by obeying the Ten Commandments" (p. 18). On another occasion, Matzat asked seventy-five members of his Bible study class who knew for sure they were going to heaven if they died tonight. Only three people raised their hands. "As a pastor, this was a devastating experience" (p. 55). The simple salvation message is difficult for people to understand, even when it is regularly preached. Hence, Matzat counsels, "When it comes to knowing the Gospel, clear teaching and repetition is necessary until eyes are opened and truth received" (p. 18).

In chap. 3, Matzat shows his Lutheran eschatology. He does not seem to distinguish between the Judgment Seat of Christ and the Great White Throne Judgment. He seems to expect a single last judgment day where believers will appear. He asks, "When you stand before God on judgment day, is it necessary that you have a perfect righteousness?" (p. 23). The correct answer is "Yes." But that righteousness comes through faith in Christ, not from your own works. People often assume that God grades on a curve, so God's actual demand for perfection needs to be emphasized: "For a person to grasp the truth of justification they must be confronted with the divine standard of perfection" (p. 24). "We may look good when compared to other people, but God does not compare us with other people. The Divine standard for holiness is God's perfect righteousness" (p. 25). If that is the standard, it should be apparent that no one measures up. Our only hope is to be justified before God by faith, apart from works.

Matzat explains that sanctification "defines how we live based on our position. It is a cooperative effort between the Christian and the Holy Spirit. The Bible teaches us to live in Christ and not in Adam" (p. 27). He continues, "Christians need to be taught how to live in Christ or abide in Christ so that they bear much fruit and experience the righteous position they have in Christ" (p. 27). Part of this teaching includes confessing God's Word, gathering around the Lord's table, and setting your mind on the Spirit (pp. 27-28).

Chapters 5 and 6 deal with the psychology of accepting the message of justification by faith apart from works. These are more difficult chapters. Matzat distinguishes between the empirical "I" and the transcendental "I." The empirical "I" is our conscious content. The degree to which we can reflect upon that content and detach ourselves from it to look at it objectively shows whether we are ready to hear the message of justification. When we hear God's demand for perfection in the Law, we must then look at our lives objectively to see if we measure up. We ought to discover that we do not live up to that demand. "By looking at the content of my consciousness through the eyes of God I am confronted with the truth that all my life and deeds are nothing before Him and that everything in me, my entire bundle of stuff, must perish eternally" (p. 41). Matzat says, "the degree to which I am willing to pass judgment on the totality of my life is the degree to which I am willing to hear and receive the Good News of the alternative righteousness of Christ" (p. 42). *JOTGES* readers will agree that is probably what normally happens when you have been evangelized with the message of justification. But that is not strictly necessary, especially if you have been evangelized with the promise of eternal life. When Jesus offered people eternal life through faith in Him, there was no apparent psychological preparation to receive that gift. People did not have to experience a twofold subjectivity where the content of their empirical "I" stood condemned before the perfect demands of God's Law. That can certainly happen, but it is not necessary to happen. The sheer graciousness of the gift of eternal life is reason enough to desire it.

Chapter 6 also describes the difference between objective and subjective justification. There are some good insights in this chapter, but also some flaws. Lutherans believe that Jesus died for all, not some: "*Objective justification* means that through the perfect life, the suffering, death and resurrection of Jesus, God forgives the sins of the entire world; imputes to the world the righteousness of Christ; and declares the world of sinners to be 'not guilty'" (p. 47). If that is true, wouldn't universalism also be true?

Matzat continues: "*Subjective justification* occurs when, as a result of the preaching of the law and the presenting of the Gospel of the blood of and righteousness of Jesus Christ, the sinner is brought to faith by the Holy Spirit and apprehends or appropriates to himself the benefits of *objective justification*, namely, the forgiveness of sins, life and salvation" (p. 48).

This reviewer does not understand the need for subjective justification if objective justification is true. If God forgives the sins of the world, what more is there to appropriate? I am forgiven. There is no need to appropriate it. I just need to believe that good news. Likewise, if God has imputed righteousness to the world, what would subjective justification add? I am already righteous. How much more righteous can I be?

This view also raises the question—why is anyone eternally lost? How can an objectively forgiven and righteous person be eternally lost?

That seems to be a contradiction. Matzat does not seem to mean that the world is only potentially forgiven and righteous, but actually so.

The problem here is that Lutheran thought takes the atonement as a "package." It fails to sufficiently distinguish between the universal and particular aspects of the benefits of the cross. The cross has different benefits for different people under different conditions. Some benefits are universal and unconditional (e.g., that Jesus takes away the sins of the world). Other benefits are conditioned on faith and only given to believers (e.g., everlasting life). Careful Bible students ought to discover which is which.

"We do not tell people you must believe and get saved or right with God. We don't have faith in our own faith. We proclaim that the world of sinners has been saved and declared to be right with God. Through this proclamation of the Law and the finished work of Christ, the Holy Spirit produces faith which grasps and apprehends the benefits of that finished work" (p. 50). Elsewhere Matzat says that it is not for him to judge whether people who have been baptized as infants but who have never believed "are going to heaven or not" (p. 57).

On the contrary, Jesus very definitely taught that you must believe to get saved or you are condemned already: "For God so loved the world that He gave His only begotten Son, that whoever believes in Him should not perish but have everlasting life...He who believes in Him is not condemned; but he who does not believe is condemned already, because he has not believed in the name of the only begotten Son of God" (John 3:16, 18). If someone has never believed, he should know he is condemned until he comes to faith. That is what Jesus taught.

JOTGES readers will appreciate this passage: "Faith is not some non-descript emotion about God nor the mere acceptance of the historical facts of the Gospels. Faith is very specific. Faith grasps the promises of God. Where you have a promise, such as the promise of the forgiveness of sins and justification, their faith is active" (p. 53). Saving faith is faith in a promise, namely, the promise that Jesus gives everlasting life to the believer.

This booklet has several very good quotes Free Grace people will find valuable. However, its understanding of the atonement and eschatology are deficient. Recommended for well-grounded believers.

Shawn Lazar
Associate Editor
Journal of the Grace Evangelical Society

Authorized: The Use & Misuse of the King James Bible. By Mark
Ward. Bellingham, WA: Lexham Press, 2018. 154 pp. Paper, $12.99.

As one who holds to the Majority Text (MT) view of textual criticism, I have a warm place in my heart for the KJV. While it follows
the Textus Receptus (TR), not the MT per se, it is still the closest
modern translation to the MT, along with the NKJV. So I was drawn
by this title.

I used the RSV until my senior year in college when I came to faith
in Christ. Then I switched to the NASB, which I used for about 15
years. After that I began to use the NKJV because of its affinity to
the MT.

Of course, Ward's experience is the opposite of mine. He grew up
with the KJV (see, e.g., pp. 19, 26, 85). He received his Ph.D. from
Bob Jones University where the KJV is "the campus standard in the
classroom and in the chapel pulpit" (bju.edu/about/positions.php). So
he has had a heavy dose of the KJV. That is what makes his comments about the KJV so helpful.

I enjoyed the discussion in chap. 1 of five things we lose if the
Church stops using the KJV. Also much appreciated was chap. 3,
"Dead Words and 'False Friends'" (pp. 29-49). He gives six major
examples of "false friends"—misleading expressions in the KJV due
to the change in meaning of the words (pp. 32-42)— and twenty-five
minor examples (pp. 45-49).

Ward's discussion of the readability of the KJV was helpful as well
(chap. 4).

I expected in this book to read a lot about the *New* KJV (NKJV).
After all, if a person was writing about the deficiencies of Windows
1.0 today, you would think he might compare it to Windows 10.
You'd certainly want to talk about the history of the various versions.

I thought Ward would compare the KJV and NKJV. What I found
instead is that he not only does not compare them, he rarely mentions
the NKJV at all! I found mention of the NKJV on only two pages
(pp. 56, 90). When he talks about the main Bible translations other
than the KJV, he omits mention of the NKJV: "People are wrong
to despise or neglect the ESV, NASB, CSB, NIV, NLT, NET Bible,
and other good evangelical Bible translations" (p. 137). When he lists
the versions he mentions the "Lexham English Bible, New American
Standard Bible, English Standard Version, Christian Standard Bible,

New International Version, NET Bible, and New Living Translation" (pp. 139-40). Those lists are the same except for the addition of the LEB.

Ward acts as though the current version of the KJV being used in churches is the 1611 edition. But it is not. Art Farstad, the head editor of the NKJV, wrote a book entitled *The New King James Version: In the Great Tradition.* He walked through the various editions and showed that the current KJV is actually the 1769 Oxford Revision (Farstad, p. 26). That revision dropped the fourteen apocryphal books which were included in the 1611 KJV (Farstad, p. 24). Ward fails to mention that fact as well. The 1769 version of the KJV, the one used today, is much changed in terms of punctuation, grammar, and spelling. It should be noted that one of its predecessors, the Cambridge edition of 1638, improved the text "by inserting words or clauses, especially in the Old Testament, overlooked by the editors of 1611" (F. H. A. Scrivener, cited by Alfred W. Pollard in *The Holy Bible 1611 Edition King James Version*, p. 52).

Here is the bottom line for Ward: since the KJV is not in vernacular English (e.g., pp. 61-86, 119, 137, 138), the KJV should not be used "for public preaching ministry, for evangelism, for discipleship materials, indeed for most situations outside individual study" (p. 137). I agree.

In terms of what version should be used, he says, "Stop looking for the 'best' English Bible. It doesn't exist. God never said it would. Take up the embarrassment of riches we now have. Make the best of our multi-translation situation, because it's a truly great problem to have" (p. 137). Here I find myself agreeing and disagreeing. I agree that we should compare English translations when we study the Bible. I do that a lot. However, I disagree that there is not a best English Bible for church pews, for evangelism and discipleship, for personal Bible reading, and for preaching and teaching. Churches certainly need to pick one version. And they should not pick by throwing a dart. They must decide what version is best. I think that best Bible is the NKJV. But that is based on my view of textual criticism, something which Ward does not discuss.

I like this book. Ward is a good writer and makes a strong case for his position. While I could have wished he included a discussion of the history of the KJV, I highly recommend *The Use & Misuse of the King James Bible*.

Robert N. Wilkin
Associate Editor
Journal of the Grace Evangelical Society

Whatever Happened to the Gospel? By R. T. Kendall. Lake Mary, FL: Charisma House, 2018. 200 pp. Paper, $15.99.

Two things attracted me to this book: the title and the author. Both are great. I loved Kendall's earlier book, *Once Saved, Always Saved*. I read this book with great expectation.

There are many things to like about this book. And there are at least a few aspects of this book that will trouble most *JOTGES* readers.

Things to like begin with his treatment of Jas 2:14-26. He is one of the only people I have read who suggests that vv 14-26 continue the discussion of how we treat the poor in our churches, Jas 2:1-13 (pp. 115-17). He suggests that the issue is not assurance of salvation (pp. 115-17). He understands the person mentioned in "Can faith save him?" not as the believer who fails to put his faith into practice, but the poor man who came into the church (Jas 2:2-6) and who was dishonored and not helped (pp. 117-18). And, he suggests that the word *justified* in Jas 2:24 should be translated as *vindicated* as some translations have in 1 Tim 3:16 (p. 119). That is all great stuff (though I still think James is referring to the indolent believer who needs saving from temporal judgment).

He talks about *hyper grace,* which he defines not as the Free Grace position, but as the teaching that says it is wrong for believers to confess our sins, that believers are already forgiven both positionally and experientially of all sins, including future ones (which is why confession is out), that believers are not under any commands, and that to suggest that we are is to put believers under the law (pp. 42-44). Then he makes this comment: "The hyper-grace people make no room for Paul's urgency that we should hope for a reward at the judgment seat of Christ (1 Cor. 9:24-27; 2 Cor. 5:10)" (p. 45).

He has one chapter on hell and one on heaven. Both are helpful.

His discussion of open theism is very brief, but excellent (pp. 46-47).

He rejects assurance by works (pp. 107-108). Super.

On the other side of the coin, his understanding of salvation in Romans is disappointing. He sees it as referring to regeneration. That leads him to misunderstand many verses in Romans, including Rom 1:16-17; 5:9 (e.g., pp. 53, 59-60).

Also disappointing is his personal testimony. He says he came to faith at age 6 (p. 9) while in an Arminian church that by his own admission taught that if a believer sinned, he lost his salvation (p. 11) and which rarely, if ever, preached the gospel (p. 11). Here is his testimony: "I knelt with my parents at their bedside and confessed my sins...I wept as I prayed. I felt a sense of peace and relief. I never looked back. I believe I was truly converted that day. But how much of the Gospel I knew at the time is another question" (p. 9). No mention of Jesus, faith in Jesus, the promise of everlasting life, etc. Strange.

Thirteen years later, on October 31, 1955, while a college student at an Arminian college, he says, "I had what I would describe as a Damascus Road experience, though it was not my conversion. It was my baptism with the Holy Spirit..." (p. 10). Kendall is a charismatic. So this statement is not too surprising. But then he continues, "I entered into a rest of faith; my heart was warmed, and peace came into my heart unlike anything I had ever experienced...My theology changed. I knew I was eternally saved, and I was given a glimpse of the sovereignty of God" (p. 10). Later in the book he says again that on October 31, 1955, "I rejoiced with unspeakable relief that I knew that I was eternally saved" (p. 151). That is an obvious testimony of the very moment at which he was born again. But no. He not only denies that assurance is of the essence of saving faith with that telling, but he suggests that one can be born again knowing little if anything about the gospel and the promise of life.

His understanding of the Greek expression *pistis Christou* is puzzling and a bit troubling as well (pp. 91-95). Most translations of that phrase read *faith in Christ,* taking *Christou* as an objective genitive. Thus Gal 2:16 would read, "a man is not justified by the works of the law but by *faith in Christ...*" (so NKJV, NASB, NIV, HCSB, NLT, ESV, CEV, RSV, NRSV, LEB). But Kendall thinks *Christou* is a subjective genitive, meaning that Christ is the subject of faith. He understands Gal 2:16 to mean that a man is justified "by the faith of Christ" (pp. 92, 94, 95). Those who hold to the new perspective on Paul translate *pistis Christou* as *Christ's faithfulness* or *the faithfulness of Christ* (only the NET Bible offers that translation). While Kendall does not suggest that translation, his explanation of what "the faith of Christ" means is unusual. He says, "By this term [*pistis Christou*] Paul means: "Christ's life (Rom. 5:10), Christ's faith (Gal. 2:20), Christ's death (Rom 5:9), Christ's resurrection (Rom. 3:25), and Christ's intercession (Heb 7:25)" (p. 94). But not one of the five verses he cites actually has *pistis Christou*. Galatians 2:20 is closest with *en pistei zō tē tou Huiou tou Theou*, "I live <u>by faith in the Son of God</u>." If we want to know what *pistis Christou* means, then we should look at places in which that expression occurs. And it always means *faith in Christ*, not the faith of Christ, whatever that would mean.

(It is, of course, true, that we are to live in light of Christ's faithfulness. But that is not expressed by the words *pistis Christou*. And that is not the meaning of Gal 2:16 or Gal 2:20.)

One of the biggest surprises in this book is Kendall's promotion of something he calls "Implicit Faith" (pp. 120-21). He does not mean by that what a Catholic would mean. Instead he understands *implicit faith* to mean a person who believes something short of the saving message yet nonetheless is born again because God views what little he believes as "a measure of knowledge that needs to be topped up at some stage" (p. 120). Kendall goes on in his discussion of implicit faith to ask if one of his liberal seminary professors who had once been a conservative will be in heaven (p. 121). He wonders about "millions of Southern Baptists, Methodists, Presbyterians, Anglicans, and Lutherans who were baptized" (p. 120). He says, "Who knows?" (p. 120). He ends that chapter (9) with the question about another man who fell away, asking, "Will he be in heaven? You tell me" (p. 121). The implication in this discussion of *implicit faith* is that most people in Christianity are born again, even if they believe in works salvation. They have *implicit faith*, and that is enough. At the very least, this is highly confusing. At worst, this leads people astray.

There are some sections that are both good and bad. He has a section entitled, "Faith Is Assurance" (pp. 105-108). That is a great title. And he makes the case that whatever we believe, we are assured is true (p. 105). Nice. But then he turns right around and says, "Being persuaded—being assured—is an essential ingredient of true faith. It is not head knowledge; it touches the heart. It is not mental assent to certain teachings" (p. 105). Confusing. Worse still, he goes on to say that "[for] faith to be *faith* is being persuaded by evidence of things *not seen* (Heb 11:1). The Queen of Sheba believed because she *saw*. But you cannot call this *faith*" (p. 106, italics his). What of the eight signs in John that are designed to lead people to faith in Christ? All belief is the result of evidence which convinces us that something is true. We never believe without evidence. We can believe things we see or things we do not see, like the existence of gravity and electricity. But whatever we believe, we believe. And we do so because the evidence has convinced us.

Finally, the last paragraph of the book is especially disappointing. Kendall ends by stating, "If you have any doubt regarding where you will spend eternity, please pray this prayer—from your heart" (p. 183). The prayer is anything but clear: "Lord Jesus Christ, I need You. I want You. I know I am a sinner, and I am sorry for my sins. Wash my sins away by Your blood. Thank You for dying on the cross for me. I repent of my sins. I welcome your Holy Spirit. As best I know how, I give You my life. Amen" (p. 183). There is no mention there of believing in Jesus or of everlasting life. Instead we find confession of sin, sorrow for sin, turning from sin, and giving one's life to Christ. That is a mild Lordship Salvation prayer.

But wait. Kendall also says this about saving faith: "It is only belief in the *heart* wherever you are—as long as the Lord Jesus Christ is the object of that faith—that is saving faith" (p. 104, italics his). A few sentences later he adds, "Saving faith is relying on the truth of the Gospel. It is believing in your heart that He died for you. It is trusting His blood, not your works. It is believing in your heart that Jesus is God, that He is the God-man. In a word, it is relying on Christ. You can only do this if you *believe in your heart*...The key: when you believe these things in your heart" (p. 105). His emphasis on believing in the heart is troubling. In addition, he says nothing there about everlasting life or the equivalent. Even so, that is a fairly good statement. It is certainly far clearer than the sinner's prayer he ends the book with.

I find this book confounding. It is an odd mix of good and bad. I recommend it for Free Grace pastors, elders, deacons, and Bible teachers. I do not recommend it for new believers or for those who are not well grounded. This book could easily confuse people.

Robert N. Wilkin
Associate Editor
Journal of the Grace Evangelical Society

Answering Christianity's Most Difficult Question—Why God Allows Us to Suffer: The Definitive Solution to the Problem of Pain and the Problem of Evil. By Kevin Tewes. Chapel Hill, NC: Triune Publishing Group, 2015.124 pp. Paper, $5.95.

The issue of why God allows suffering is an important one. I read this book, hoping to get some good insights into the problem. I came away disappointed.

I was put off by the author suggesting that his book is "the definitive solution" (pp. iii, 14) and that all other explanations provide "flimsy, worn-out arguments" (p. vi). Does Tewes really provide "an entirely new and comprehensive solution" (p. 13)? One reviewer, Christopher Ray, put it well in his Amazon review: "The first thing that stands out in Tewes' book is an undercurrent of hubris that spoils even his most savory statements with an aftertaste of pomposity."

Another review, this one by Dr. Gregory Schulz of Concordia University Wisconsin (available online) makes a similar comment at the start of the review: "Ladies and gentlemen of the jury, this book, from its hubristic title to its concluding unphilosophical postscript-ing of Soren Kierkegaard, ought to be ruled inadmissible to the discussion of the Problem of Evil. It is not serious. It is not philosophical. It is not theological."

I was also put off by the way in which Tewes hides his thesis. He talks about this exciting new solution to the problem. Yet where does he state this solution?

I thought I missed it, so I consulted other reviews to see if others could determine the thesis. Finally I found one reviewer who stated the author's solution (in his own words), yet without giving any page references. That helped me find the supposedly new solution of Tewes:

love (see pp. 99-112). The author wrongly thinks that, "The central purpose of creation is to allow for the experience of love" (p. 82). Since that is true, "God judges that it is better to preserve mankind's ability to experience love than it is to spare man from the myriad kinds of pain that result from the misuse of his power" (p. 82).

Tewes sees only two options: "In other words, God can shelter each human being from the negative consequences of the decision-making of other humans, or he can instead allow humans to maintain their power to affect one another through their actions" (pp. 81-82).

There are three problems with this solution. First, the purpose of creation is not anthropocentric. Man was created for God's good pleasure. The purpose of creation is to please God (2 Cor 5:9; Rev 22:3-5). God wished to create beings who would love and serve Him. While humans are and will forever be greatly blessed by God if they come to faith in Christ, the creation's central purpose is the rule and joy of God (Heb 12:2). Second, it is not true that if God limited man's ability to hurt one another, then we would be unable to love. God limits our ability to hurt one another every hour of every day. Until the Tribulation, God greatly restrains evil (2 Thess 2:6-7). We may think we have free will. But in reality, God restricts our free will. Who knows how much pain and suffering each of us have escaped because God restrained others from hurting us further? Third, even if God completely eliminated our ability to sin, we would still be able to love. We won't sin in Jesus' kingdom. Yet forever we will love and be loved. Tewes fails to explain why the kingdom has not come yet. Suffering will be minimal during the Millennium and nonexistent on the new earth (Rev 21:4). So why didn't Jesus simply return earlier? Second Peter 3:9 (see also vv 1-12) gives that answer. But Tewes does not consider 2 Pet 3:9.

There is no exegesis of Scripture in this book. That is disturbing for a book which presumably is on Christian apologetics. Even proof texting is rarely done. On only nine pages in the text does the author even quote or mention a verse or passage (i.e., pp. 18, 19, 59, 62, 68, 69, 85, 105, 105; he also mentions Scripture texts in footnotes on pp. 77, 106 and in some of the endnotes on pp. 116, 117, 120, 121).

I am not a philosopher or an apologist. However, Tewes's supposedly new and definitive solution to the problem of evil is not new to me. While he takes a slightly different slant on the free-will solution, I've heard variations of this view my entire Christian experience.

I do not recommend this book. It fails to deliver what the title and subtitle offer.

Robert N. Wilkin
Associate Editor
Journal of the Grace Evangelical Society

Doubt, Faith, and Certainty. By Anthony C. Thiselton. Grand Rapids, MI: Eerdmans, 2017. 160pp. Paper, $20.00.

Thiselton is a professor at the University of Nottingham in England and is a well-known NT scholar. The title of this book caught my eye. I was interested in how Thiselton defined faith and whether he felt a believer could have assurance or certainty of eternal life.

Unfortunately, this book does not really deal with the issue of assurance of salvation. Instead it deals with faith and assurance in a philosophical way and how they relate to Christian living in a more general way. It can be safe to say, however, that Thiselton does not believe in complete assurance. When it comes to the meaning of "faith" and any "certainty" that accompanies a person's faith, Thiselton says that there are a number of different meanings of both terms. In fact, he refers to the three terms in the book's title as being "polymorphous" (p. 10).

Throughout the book Thiselton maintains that doubt is not necessarily a bad thing. We all have doubt in this life, but it does not mean that one has a lack of faith. Instead, it can be a good thing because it can lead to an attitude of humility and a deeper search for the things of God, as well as self-criticism (p. 3). It can "stimulate us to fresh thought and questioning" (p. vii). In fact, doubt can lead to faith (p. 2), as well as a more "authentic view of God" (p. 5). Thiselton says that the man who asks Jesus to help his unbelief (Mark 9:24) shows that doubt and belief can exist at the same time. The man believes but also does not believe (p. 44). The same thing can be said about the prophet Jonah in the book that bears his name.

Thiselton points out that in the Scriptures, and especially in the Psalms, there are candid expressions of doubt and questioning which show up on a regular basis (pp. 40, 54). They are simply part of the life of faith. While all believers have doubt, the "isolated" believer is more subject to it (p. 36). The more we are a part of a community of believers, the less doubt we are likely to have.

The book looks in depth at the different views of faith, doubt, and certainty among philosophers, psychologists, ethicists, and even medieval thinkers, including Catholic scholars (e.g., pp. 19ff). Thiselton has a long discussion on the role that reason plays in faith and concludes that reason does have a part in what a person believes. Faith can be seen as something reached with the help of reason based upon the "probability" of its being true (p. 58). He does not believe reason alone can bring a person to faith, but reason is a gift from God in order that we might believe (p. 74). The relationship between faith, doubt, and reason is very complicated (p. 92).

For Thiselton, certainty is intimately related to the "eschaton." It is only when the believer sees God, will certainty be possible. Until that time, the believer must live with uncertainty and doubt. But this, too, is a good thing in Thiselton's view, as it causes the believer to have faith in God's wisdom and goodness and to patiently wait for the day when doubt will be replaced by certainty. Thiselton says that many of the parables of Jesus speak of the ambiguity and doubt that we have in the present, which is to be resolved on that future day (p.135).

As far as the relationship of certainty with the eschaton, Thiselton says we are to become what we are. In this life we are fallible and uncertain, but what the Christian will become is "provisionally" certain. Only in the light of the end does the revelation of God become fully understandable. The only way a Christian could have complete certainty now would require knowing all of history, which is impossible (pp. 127-28).

For Thiselton, only the kingdom of God provides certainty because it "cannot be shaken" (p. 137). In this life, certainty is distorted because of sin. A measure of distortion should not take us by surprise (p. 139). Simply put, certainty in this life is impossible because certainty is based upon sight.

Thiselton says in this life faith can mean many things. To claim to have certainty in spiritual areas may mask a "degree of arrogance" (p. viii.).

In some places, Thiselton does discuss the Scripture. He says that in the Bible the word faith has at least thirteen definitions. It can be synonymous with John's use of "abiding." But in other places in the NT (pp. 10-11), it can also mean faithfulness and obedience as well.

There are also two types of certainty in a philosophical sense. There is a subjective certainty, such as when Paul says he is convinced of something (Phil 1:6). But Thiselton says there is an objective certainty, which the Christian can claim, based upon God's propositions (p. 16). However, neither of these provides complete assurance.

When he gives the many meanings of faith, Thiselton is aware of the Lordship Salvation definition of saving faith even though he does not call it that. He says that one use of the word faith involves "performance" (p. 42). I found it interesting that Lordship Salvation adherents would probably feel comfortable with this view of faith.

Readers of the *JOTGES* will find Thiselton's discussion of faith in the Gospel of John interesting. He recognizes that John uses different prepositions with the verb "believe" and that the phrases mean to trust or believe "in" (or "on") Jesus. However, he does not see the permanent reception of eternal life as a result of that faith. Instead, faith is a moment by moment thing in the Gospel of John (pp. 63-64).

Many will not accept one of the major premises of the discussions in this book. Thiselton does not accept that the Bible is the inspired Word of God, even though he does not specifically state it. Those who believe in the inspiration of the Scriptures can have certainty in this life, based upon what the Bible says. Those who believe in the inspiration of the Bible would not consider having assurance in the propositions of God as a sign of arrogance. For example, it is not arrogant for the believer to have certainty about having eternal life, because the believer takes Jesus at His word.

Others will certainly take exception with Thiselton's view that faith and doubt can exist at the same time. James tells us that this is not possible and that the man who doubts does not believe God and should not expect to receive from God what he asks for (James 1). One can indeed have faith and doubt at the same time, but not in regards to the same proposition. The man in Mark 9 believed some things about Christ, but did not believe other things about Him. That is how he could have faith and doubt at the same time.

Thiselton's many definitions of faith can be confusing. "Abiding" in John's writings does not deal with faith. Instead, it speaks about having fellowship with God by keeping His commandments. This is not the same thing as believing something.

This book is not an easy read. It is heavy in philosophical discussions. It quotes from writers such as Plantinga, Pannenberg, Kant, Bultmann, and Aquinas. For readers who want to know what the Bible says as the result of exegesis about faith and certainty, this is not the book for them. However, if somebody wants to know how secular thinkers or theologians who do not have a high view of inspiration see faith and certainty, I would recommend this book.

Kenneth W. Yates
Editor
Journal of the Grace Evangelical Society

The Gospel of John. Catholic Commentary on Sacred Scripture. By Francis Martin and William M. Wright IV. Grand Rapids, MI: Baker Academic, 2015. 366 pp. Paper, $24.99.

The average Free Grace believer may see no reason for acquiring this book. However, knowing how Catholic priests are likely to explain John's Gospel can be quite helpful. To those lacking a Catholic background, statements by priests or other in-the-know Catholics about John's Gospel are often surprising. Martin and Wright's commentary contains many such affirmations. A pattern emerges: Statement 1 affirms a Biblical truth (that seems non-Catholic). Soon afterward, Statement 2 avows a point of Catholic dogma which contradicts the first. Highlighting these statements would be helpful (one color for a Biblical affirmation, another for the contradictory assertion from dogma). Sometimes the authors add words to make Statement 1 seem to affirm dogma (these could be highlighted with the color used for dogma).

Examples of truth interspersed with error follow.

In commenting upon John 3:16-17, Statement 1 is fine: "We accept this gift [salvation/eternal life] through faith in Jesus." Statement 2 is false Church dogma: "Faith is yielding to the Spirit, who first moves a person to assent to what God has revealed and *to commit one's whole life to God* [a footnote refers the readers to Catechism 150, 153]." (p. 74, emphasis added).

Comments upon John 5:24 indicate a recognition that believers receive eternal life on earth prior to physical death. Other than the gratuitous characterization of faith as "yielding faith," the statement is good:

> This hearing, believing, and having eternal life all take place *now*, in the present moment, as does the passing from death to life, and it has future effects. One's present response in yielding faith to Jesus leads to a future freedom from condemnation. We must still pass through bodily death, but we will do so as those already possessing eternal life (p. 105).

Despite this statement, the authors do not recognize that the moment that one believes in Jesus Christ for everlasting life, he/she has life everlasting. Thus, their comment on John 2:11b is:

> They [His disciples] are able to see the Cana miracle as a sign, and now, moving beyond a series of affirmations, they begin to believe in Jesus personally. Faith goes beyond assent to doctrinal claims, moving to a personal commitment of trust in God himself. As we shall see, the disciples' faith remains imperfect throughout the Gospel (see John 13–16). It reaches maturity only after Jesus' resurrection, with the assistance of the Holy Spirit (p. 60).

In other words, every believer (in theory) receives everlasting life during this lifetime, but (in practice) the faith of none of those that John's Gospel says believed in Him actually "reached maturity" before Jesus' resurrection. If no one could have a matured faith and everlasting life until after Jesus' resurrection, would not John 5:24 be bait-and-switch? Jesus did not say that eternal life would come to the believer when his/her faith reached maturity.

Similarly, in commenting on Martha's confession (John 11:27), they say, "Martha has a great deal of faith in Jesus, but like the other disciples thus far, hers is not yet fully mature (see 11:39-40)" (p. 205). Their comment upon her faith as immature is: "She may believe that Jesus has the divine power to resurrect the dead on the last day, but she does not realize he can revive the dead now" (p. 210). Apparently, Martin and Wright think that Martha lacked eternal life because she did not yet believe that He would raise Lazarus. A few moments after this conversation with Jesus, He raised Lazarus (11:44). Would the authors then grant that Martha had a mature faith and everlasting life? Probably not. Jesus had not yet been resurrected, so they would still claim that her faith was immature.

Reading Martin and Wright's commentary is an "up and down" experience. They reject much liberal thought. They often affirm Biblical truth, even if fleetingly. However, they are so steeped in Catholic Church dogma that they engage regularly in Orwellian double-speak. Readers who are not well grounded in grace may not detect the bipolar self-contradictions inherent in any attempt to expound John's message of life, while accepting the *nihil obstat*. This phrase signifies that nothing contained within would hinder one from Catholic doctrine and practice. As a result, the *nihil obstat* means that much contained within does hinder one from Biblical doctrine and practice. Despite the *nihil obstat*, though, one will find in this commentary something that rarely appears in other Catholic books: a number of direct admissions that John's Gospel proclaims faith alone in Jesus Christ alone for eternal life (see the discussion of Statement-1 [what God says] versus Statement-2 [what human dogma says] pronouncements earlier in this review). This may help our Catholic friends to see that Jesus says what He means about the gift of everlasting life.

How we mourn for those entangled in a system that hinders seeing faith alone in Jesus Christ alone for everlasting life. One passes from death to life by believing Jesus Christ for His promise of life everlasting. Contra Martin and Wright, God wants people to know that they have passed from death to life.

John Niemelä
President
Message of Life Ministries

Made in the USA
Middletown, DE
23 December 2018